Chocolate Covered Money

SECRETS OF THE MARKETING GENIUS
WHO BUILT THE WORLD'S MOST
SUCCESSFUL CHOCOLATE BRANDS

BRAD YATER

Post Hill Press

A POST HILL PRESS BOOK
ISBN: 978-1-63758-807-9
ISBN (eBook): 978-1-63758-808-6

Chocolate Covered Money:
Secrets of the Marketing Genius Who Built the World's Most Successful Chocolate Brands

Cover design by Conroy Accord

All people, locations, events, and situations are portrayed to the best of the author's memory. While all of the events described are true, many names and identifying details have been changed to protect the privacy of the people involved.

Post Hill Press
New York • Nashville
posthillpress.com

Published in the United States of America
1 2 3 4 5 6 7 8 9 10

CONTENTS

PREFACE

The odds were not in my favor. But that's what makes it such a good story.

The world knows Godiva because of me.

I took Godiva to the top of the jet-set world of high-end chocolates, stopping at nothing to remain number one.

I was enticed to manage an even bigger Belgian brand, Leonidas Chocolate, enabling me to fulfill the master plan of owning my own company, KC Chocolatier.

If someone had predicted I'd have a galaxy of stars as customers, I would have said they have the wrong Brad Yater.

Everyone will see a bit of themselves in me, because we all love chocolate... and money.

Chapter 1

DEPOSIT ALL THE MONEY IN MY BANK ACCOUNT

I made it my destiny to create a global brand. I am the only American in history to have managed all three of Belgium's three biggest luxury chocolate brands—Godiva, Leonidas, and KC Chocolatier. The story that follows in *Chocolate Covered Money* reveals how that happened to me of all people.

I love retailing, and I love chocolates, so this book is intended as a tell-all about my impact on marketing as it shapes brands. Anyone who wants to know what working in the chocolate business is like will see behind the curtain. Good marketing is, in fact, the secret sauce, not just good chocolate.

I've always had a sweet tooth. Even as a youngster, dessert was my favorite part of the meal. As a young boy, I remember spending my entire allowance buying penny candy at the candy counter of Bloomingdale's. As soon as I was old enough to pick out teacher's gifts, I always selected an assorted box of chocolates because that's what I would have wanted to receive as a present.

Growing up, I became fascinated by money. For some reason the subject of money mattered to me, at an age when other kids were worried about their favorite sports teams' scores. I vaguely sensed that whatever it meant to be financially successful required being a businessman working at a company.

I decided to major in business at college, attending Rollins College in Winter Park, Florida. That is where this story begins, as a chain of events sent me down the path to working with—and eventually for—Godiva Chocolate.

Upon graduating with an MBA in 1984, I joined the management training program at Federated Department Stores without knowing where I would be assigned upon completing the three-month retail training course. Retail historians will remember the 1980s as the golden age of department stores. During that era, Federated had recruited heavy hitters to run the various nameplates. I had an opportunity to work alongside and get to know industry veterans including Howard Socol, who went on to become CEO of Barneys, and David Scheiner, the future President of Jordan Marsh and Macy's.

When, to my pleasant surprise, an opening came up in Miami at the end of summer, I gladly counted my lucky stars and accepted. I was assigned to work in the housewares and gourmet food buying office, sourcing inventory for twenty-seven locations in the Florida divisions of Burdines and Bloomingdale's, all along the East Coast. In that role, I had a million-dollar annual budget to stock the branch stores. Federated carried Godiva Chocolate products, and my job was to make the relationship profitable. I instinctively considered Godiva to be a "diamond-in-the-rough" that could be polished for everyone's enjoyment.

My first order of business was to figure out how chocolate could become a year-round business. The problem was that previous buyers had turned a full-time job into a part-time job. Chocolate shipments came in decorated for Christmas, Valentine's Day, and Easter. Stores displayed Godiva on temporary fixturing placed in the middle of the marble aisle walkways. The rest of the year, the temporary fixturing used for Godiva displays was taken down. While other products we carried, such as cookies, cakes, and dried fruits and nuts, seemed best suited for major holidays, chocolates performed well as a day-in-day-out merchandise category.

Whether it was Burdines or Godiva that was mismanaged, or a little of both, I brought the parties together, and immediately things began to change. Soon, I was organizing a regional roll out. It is very hard now, thinking back, to imagine a time when Godiva wasn't everywhere. In 1984, Burdines only had refrigerated candy counters at the main store in Dadeland. Since chocolate must be displayed in a chilled display case, due to the fact that the air conditioning in department stores turns off at night, individual chocolates sold by the piece were not available at the branches. Federated did not yet have refrigerated trucks, and there was no cool room at the warehouse. How could we put together a program to get our best seller into all doors for sale year-round? Apparently, none of my predecessors had thought to call Godiva and ask for *their* ideas on accomplishing statewide distribution.

My first introduction to Godiva was when my Godiva account executive, Brandy, who was Godiva's point person handling Florida, showed up at my fifth-floor office in the downtown Miami store at 22 East Flagler Street with high energy and a sparkling, effervescent personality. Brandy was dressed professionally in a two-piece navy-blue suit. I later found out Godiva's sales force was all female, and their "look" was exactly this: very corporate but with a little sex appeal thrown in, somewhat reminiscent of Lady Godiva herself.

Before the meeting could begin, I had to ask about the other thing I noticed. "Why are you carrying around a big white cardboard carton that has a handle on it?" I asked.

Brandy explained, "It's a standard-issue Godiva sample case, and all the Godiva reps carry them." It was Godiva's version of a briefcase, one filled with truffles for me to taste and packaging samples for me to see.

We discussed my vision for what had to happen next. I described to Brandy a system that we could put in place in partnership, revolutionizing Godiva's distribution and exploding both parties' profits. I wanted a new style of Godiva display case that would allow customers to reach in and help themselves to prepacked boxes of chocolates. Gone would be the days of a salesclerk behind the counter hand packing each box of chocolate for customers. That was too low volume. I expected Godiva to pack the boxes and ribbon them at the factory, shipping gifts ready to display on branded self-service fixtures.

In order to transport the chocolate to the stores, I overhauled Godiva's logistics. By switching to third-party delivery services, Godiva could ship directly to each branch store using two-to-three-day shipping by air. Godiva would build shipping costs into the wholesale price. (Both parties agreed that we could increase Godiva's retail price to customers to cover the added cost of shipping.) I budgeted a first-year commitment, totaling a few-hundred-thousand-dollars guarantee. On that basis, Godiva was willing to pay for the purchase and installation of new self-service refrigerated chocolate counters.

By the end of my second year in the buying office, Federated was Godiva's number one wholesale account in the US. We purchased over $1 million worth of chocolate at cost and sold it for over $2 million at retail, earning a $1 million gross margin equaling fifty points. Federated then rolled out similar programs at other divisions, such as Bullock's in Los Angeles, Rich's in Atlanta, and Lazarus in Ohio.

Finding ways to sell more chocolate at Burdines also meant I was increasing Godiva's sales. At first, I did not see the long-term significance of what I was doing, but soon the unexpected happened in the form of a retail bankruptcy: Federated declared Chapter 11 in 1987 for the first of many times.

Brandy called me. "What are you going to do?" she asked. "Well, my paycheck bounced, so that's not a good sign," I confided. Brandy later told me she had relayed our conversation all the way up to the shareholders' representative in Brussels.

The next week I received a call from Godiva's owners, a secretive brother-sister duo. The family had acquired Godiva as a growth play. The shareholders were not interested in merely sustaining the company; they wanted to grow the company significantly. Both were aware of my reputation as a cheerleader for the Belgian chocolate industry. It was made clear that neither was directly involved in daily management, but in this case, they asked for what they called a "knowledge transfer."

I could pitch to the shareholders everything I thought Godiva could do to position itself as a leading global brand, how much I estimated it would cost, and what the returns would be. The details could fill another book, but for purposes of getting to what happened next, we met outside Philadelphia at a hotel in Conshohocken, near the Godiva factory. (Godiva Chocolates that were sold in the US were manufactured in Philadelphia. Godiva Chocolates sold in Europe were made in Brussels.)

For this special occasion, I wore a white double-breasted blazer by Christian Dior with dark slacks, a taupe shirt and matching tie, and Prada shoes. On the way, I stopped at my safe deposit box to get out the good jewelry, a Rolex watch and Mont Blanc pen, so that I would be taken seriously when meeting Godiva's majority shareholders.

The brother was tall and athletic with an outgoing personality, and he carried himself with an air of East Coast country club good manners and congeniality. The sister was from horse country, exquisitely coiffed, and could have easily been mistaken for a mid-western housewife rather than a person on Forbes top-ten wealthiest list, as they both were. I found out they were both Americans; she lived outside of Tampa, and he lived in Philadelphia.

Here just the three of us sat in a hospitality suite on a cold winter day, with snow swirling around the plate glass windows, sipping tea and making introductions. He locked his eyes on me as if to drive home the point that I had the floor and had better not have called a meeting that would turn out to be a waste of his time. She cocked her head and tried to form a slight smile through tightly pursed lips, a nonchalant signal silently daring me not to fumble. I knew I had to speak directly and with no ambiguity. There was no way I could risk them leaving the room without understanding the power of my formula.

I used the opportunity to describe in broad strokes what they would get if they paid for my services.

Wasting no time for chit chat, I dove right in, describing my master plan for building their asset into a global behemoth.

"Start opening Godiva stores," I began, "control the retail environment, take charge of the brand experience, and depend less on third parties for retail points of sale. If I had a budget of $20 million and twenty people, we would develop, launch, and build Godiva boutiques. We will license out the name to make products like liquor and ice cream, develop brand extensions such as coffee, hot chocolate, and cookies, and expand overseas." They both nodded, not saying anything. "Your valuation will be $1 billion," was my closing remark. They looked at each other and said, "Let's work out a deal."

Within a weekend, from Friday afternoon to the following Monday morning, I went from being a buyer of chocolate to selling chocolate. I worked for Godiva for the next thirteen years as an executive in the North American division, taking the firm's sales from $50 million to $350 million in that time. While I was not a founder of Godiva, I was the first generation of outside leadership the family investors brought in to lead the company.

I set about building a brand—not just selling chocolate—which requires two different skill sets. Eventually I moved to Los Angeles because California is the epicenter of the luxury chocolate industry in the US. This made it easier for me to attract the top marketing team in the retail world at the time. Short term, I set about selling chocolate by focusing on marketing to gain market share and increase profits.

Long term, what I had in mind, as a person who thinks big, was to make Godiva a household name on every continent. Building the brand took precedence over getting involved in the minutiae of competing with other chocolatiers to come out with whatever new trend was hot at the moment. Godiva under my direction would stay the course as an aspirational luxury brand positioned at the top of the category. If competitors raised their price point, I increased Godiva prices even more.

I believe what is meant by the term "corporate culture" is that companies are formed and influenced by the mindset of the personalities that run them. Ultimately the saying, "there are more chocoholics than alcoholics" proved true, because the G-rated nature of multi-generational appeal helped make not only the Godiva brand but the entire chocolate category the monster it is today. I don't know if I could have pulled off this phenomenon marketing dill pickles.

Ultimately a business is only a hobby if it does not make money. "With volume comes profit," is my mantra because I stop at nothing to increase volume. Look at it any way you want—some people refer to being a "category killer," others call it "product development" or "industry disruption"—but as sales figures increase, bottom line net profit materializes, even at poorly run operations or inexperienced startups. I have the confidence to use investors' capital to implement my business plan in order to provide sizable returns to shareholders. Making a profit needs to be the goal of starting or running a business, otherwise people need to ask themselves what their motivation is for putting in the time and effort.

Over the next decade through the 1980s and 1990s, I proceeded to take the mystery out of marketing. Godiva was the perfect seasonal business to test different ways to market. Christmas came and went, Valentine's came and went, and then Easter came and went—every year. Each sales cycle had a finite marketing budget. Tracking measurable results was easy because we took inventory. I would know within six weeks how well each season's marketing efforts worked. Once I had each season's formula down, it was just a matter of "rinse and repeat."

Godiva's US store count peaked at 250 boutiques. The shareholders earned $10 million a year while implementing my business plan. As a Fortune 500 company publicly traded on the New York Stock Exchange, Godiva's share price hit $67 and split several times as IPOs were offered for other divisions that were spun off (Vlasic Pickles: 1998) and sold (Mrs. Paul's: 1996).

Godiva is now a household name on every continent. A lot happened along the way, and there are some fascinating business lessons to relate. Most people who meet me ask what was the best part of working at Godiva. I answer by saying "Godiva made me realize that you can never have enough money," because what I learned early on at Godiva is that the more money a company earns, the more it is able to accomplish for its people. This book is about making sure your business makes enough to take care of you.

Chapter 2

USE IT OR LOSE IT

My business plans form the foundation for very recognizable companies. First, I position products to have widespread appeal. Then, I give the brand its own personality as the first step towards writing a business plan as a "brand bible." From there, I structure the process for monetizing the everlasting cultural appeal of what is to become a brand beloved for its personality.

I re-positioned Godiva from what it had been, one of many foreign chocolate companies competing for shelf space, to what it became under my direction, the leader in super-premium "gifts in good taste." That specifically meant two things: I priced Godiva above all other chocolates, and I emphasized recognizable packaging to make Godiva giftable. In other words, my job was to make sure Godiva was going to compete as a gifting brand, not a chocolate food.

Godiva would come to stand for "good taste." That was Godiva's personality in a nutshell. And by "taste," I do not mean flavor; I am referring to the brand reflecting a classy, special-occasion, gourmet, European luxury "image," all at the same time. If

Lady Godiva was a person alive today, in my mind she would be living in a Fifth Avenue penthouse, supported by a trust fund after having graduated from finishing school. That was the upscale feeling I was aspiring to.

Having defined Godiva's personality, next I wrote Godiva's business plan. Business plans outline ways in which the company will succeed. Business plans begin with a sentence, known as a "mission statement," defining the company's goal. Godiva's mission statement was "to become the world's finest luxury chocolate brand." Notice the mission statement sentence did not end after the word "chocolate." Including the word "brand" in the mission statement was significant because I was not just selling chocolate, I was building a brand. Those are two completely different skill sets. The sales force could sell more chocolate if I could figure out ways to make the chocolate a more desirable brand. Godiva needed to be a recognizable brand for it to someday be sold for a billion-dollar valuation because buyers pay premiums to acquire brands. (At the time, Godiva was not a brand yet; it was a manufacturer.)

My thinking was so out-of-the-box that I began to transition Godiva from being a manufacturer to being a retailer. How many companies have done that before? Well, we were among the first. It was possible because of the flexibility left open in the business plan enabling Godiva to both sell chocolate (wholesaling to department stores) and to build its brand (by controlling its own environment in Godiva owned-and-operated retail stores).

There is a retail saying, "the brand experience is the store experience." A store defines a brand by virtue of its architecture, signage, merchandising displays, and service model. I do not get the sense that people feel as connected to, or as emotional about, virtual brands sold online, as they do about brands they may interact with in a store, with salespeople, and with other customers.

When people ask what I do, I say that the primary skill I have is the ability to put my finger on the pulse of what has commercial appeal. I look at a package design from the standpoint of me being the arbiter of good taste (meaning I must agree the Godiva customer will like it). Packaging I deem to be great makes it to market while the rest are cancelled. Beyond its individually packaged products, with its own flagship stores (which we referred to as "boutiques"), Godiva becoming a retail brand meant that Godiva's marketing soon started targeting both Godiva products *and* Godiva stores.

Godiva boutiques cost about $250,000 each to build at the time. Malls provided foot traffic, which naturally drove sales since chocolate is an impulse purchase. Financially, each store generated enough profit on average to pay for itself in two years. Once construction costs were recouped, a portion of net profits were reinvested into building more stores. This cycle of expansion enabled Godiva boutiques to do triple duty: stores sold product, operated as incubators to gain a sense of what products people wanted, and served as billboards for the brand.

Godiva's annual construction budget allocated $3 million for building flagship stores. This allocation was "use it or lose it," meaning that if the budget was not fully spent, reserves did not carry over into the next fiscal year. Team bonuses and raises were set to help achieve performance targets of roughly one new Godiva store opening per month. But not really—because the last thing I wanted to do was open an under-performing store.

On the one hand, I wanted Godiva's real estate strategy to be known in the retail industry as Godiva being approachable about considering prime locations that became available. On the other hand, we would say "no" a lot when contacted by developers. That is because I kept a list of places where Godiva needed to be. The organization was on the lookout for development opportunities in those neighborhoods on my list. For the rest of the country, Godiva would have had to spend too much money on marketing to ramp up local demand. Returns on investment needed to be quite rapid.

The origins of my list were simple. Godiva took our cues from where Neiman Marcus and Saks Fifth Avenue built stores. Those cities became more or less the focus of our expansion as a guide for where we could draw our type of customers. South Coast Plaza in Orange County was the first stop for many European fashion brands wanting to try out a mall. Godiva found South Coast clientele to be "aspirational," seeking conspicuous consumption. Precisely the opposite was Copley Place in Back Bay Boston, where families traced origins back to the Mayflower. Copley Place was used as a place to test Godiva's appeal to understated New Englanders.

Godiva used demographic short-hand to describe stores: suburban mothers (Short Hills in New Jersey), Southern entertaining (North Park in Charlotte), Latin America (Dadeland in Miami), middle America (Beachwood in Cleveland), money to burn (King of Prussia in Philadelphia), inner-urban (Michigan Avenue in Chicago), connoisseurs (Menlo Park in San Francisco), corporate gifting (Tyson's Corner in Virginia), tourists (Ala Moana in Honolulu), retirees (Biltmore in Scottsdale), and top rung (the Galleria in St. Louis).

A construction company based in Nashville built all of Godiva's shops. Many leases had to be in development simultaneously to keep twelve stores coming down the pipeline at any given time. Although everything went through me, and I had to personally sign off on every location, near the end of each fiscal year, the site selection process became decision by committee.

High on my list of criteria was the objective of bringing Godiva to "fashion" malls, as opposed to "headquarters" malls. This is an industry way of saying "high end" versus "mainstream." Occasionally, Godiva wound up building a store in a headquarters mall because I did not want to forego spending the remaining "use it or lose it" budget when there were no prime fashion mall locations available as options during a particular year.

This was the case with Fashion Fair in Fresno. I knew Fresno would turn out to be a low-volume location, but it would at least bring in some volume, and as a manufacturer operating as a retailer, the incremental volume would only help to lower our average unit costs of production. As expected, Fresno ranked number 250 out of 250 stores on every year's sales report.

But the location in California's "wheat belt" was still profitable. Fashion Fair wanted to elevate their center and offered Godiva a good deal. In my opinion a retail store cannot be profitable unless the lease is negotiated favorably from the outset. No amount of marketing or management talent after the fact will be able to overcome a cost structure that is too high, or a location with too many competitors, poor visibility, or difficult accessibility. During the negotiating stage, each store is set up for success with prime visibility and phased rent (rent that begins low and gradually increases over time). I would walk away from a potential site when my retail instincts told me the rent would be too high based on the level of sales expected by not having enough of our clientele living and working in the trade area.

In hindsight, the reason I think talented real estate industry veterans liked what we were doing was because they were hooking their cabooses onto my gravy train. I laser-focused Godiva's growth into regions with suitable demographics, and mall landlords took credit for that success to a certain extent by sending out press releases making it sound like Godiva desperately pursued a location in their mall. But that is what they got paid to do—manage their assets on behalf of ownership, which was typically a REIT (a commercial entity called a real estate investment trust) such as Macerich in the case of Fresno.

Based on my experience, the science of demographics was startlingly accurate. So, what were Godiva's demographics specifically? For purposes of site selection, we targeted six indices: a.) high-income neighborhoods with b.) above-average levels of disposable income, c.) population growth, d.) growth in income, e.) growth in population density, and f.) an even mix of residents, tourists, and businesses.

The profile of Godiva's core customer was a woman with children, a college graduate, employed as a professional, earning over $120,000 per year, who travels extensively, and buys the very best for her family, whether it is olive oil, champagne, or chocolate, who is a repeat customer and refers Godiva to friends often. The long-term goal was to add one more trait or characteristic: "and who grew up eating Godiva." But Godiva was still too young of a brand to be able to say that, so we needed to wait for a generation.

Ideally suitable retail sites are hard to find. When a great site becomes available, every national retail concept competes for it. I held back some budget to be able to sign leases in an "A" mall Godiva needed to be in if the opportunity suddenly arose. Budgeting was a balancing act because with malls, timing is everything. If Godiva hesitated, and the mall landlord signed a competitor, Godiva typically would be locked out for ten years due to non-compete clauses. Brand-building could be set back a decade in a growing part of a city where our marketing reached Godiva's target audience who'd then only be able to find us in department stores with a limited selection.

By the late 1990's, Godiva had become a forty-dollar-per-pound product line in part because of price increases necessitated due to the cost of marketing. With the goal of generating more sales per square foot out of the top performing stores, underperforming boutiques that had not been remodeled were closed.

Some demographics Godiva tried to appeal to did not work so well: boom towns (Charleston, Birmingham), heartland (Omaha, Kansas City, Little Rock), pockets of wealth (Santa Barbara, Old Hyde Park in Tampa), up-and-coming (Providence), and Canada cross-border shoppers (Buffalo).

These cities are mostly in the Midwest, where people are more conservative about spending money, or in smaller cities where people may have less disposable income. I don't know the reasons, but we did not spend too much time analyzing the decision to close a store. Remodeling would not have been a good return on investment in these stores.

Then there were places I knew Godiva could not make money opening stores based on the population and income figures I was shown. There has never been a Godiva store in fourteen states: Montana, Kentucky, Alaska, New Hampshire, Delaware, Maine, Idaho, West Virginia, Mississippi, Iowa, Vermont, North Dakota, South Dakota, and Wyoming.

I did decide to test the concept of Godiva "clearance" stores in cities without a flagship boutique so as not to cannibalize business or tarnish the brand. Since other retailers offering a menu of consumable foodstuffs in outlet malls were selling at full price, I expected Godiva to be able to do the same. But off-price customers did not understand Godiva's product offering. Clearance shops became more about clearing out discontinued boxes and ribbons than about selling high volumes of luxury chocolate.

The experiment turned out to be a rare marketing misstep, and these shops all closed. It turns out there is a big difference between Cinnabon and Orange Julius selling self-consumption foods at full retail versus Godiva selling what were perceived as past-season/discontinued/clearance food gifts at full retail. I thought we could do the volume by selling individual pieces of chocolate, but outlet customers did not want to invest the time selecting their own assortment, or perhaps the public in these relatively rural markets did not appreciate fine chocolates, or they were not willing to pay Godiva's premium prices for gourmet chocolate.

Ultimately, the pathway for Godiva became clear: grow in big cities on both coasts. We built six stores in New York, ten stores in Los Angeles, and multiple shops in Miami and Chicago. All of these locations (but one) were company owned and operated. Each Godiva branch made a daily bank deposit locally under our policy of "money in the bank." At midnight, the bank's computer electronically "swept" all the money up from hundreds of local accounts and transferred it to Godiva's corporate master account, where bills were paid. Gross profit margins were 70 percent and net profits averaged about 20 percent of sales. The specialty food industry target was to achieve 15 to 20 percent net profit per door, putting Godiva on the high end of performers landlords had to choose from.

These numbers help explain why so many retailers struggle. Their cost of goods is too high. Godiva manufactured its own inventory. That meant we could control manufacturing costs. There were no middlemen in our supply chain. Going high-end created even more spread.

Meanwhile, Godiva had also begun opening identical shops in Europe and Asia, where I would go for training. New Godiva store managers in other countries asked how we differentiated ourselves against competing chocolatiers in their neighborhoods. The way I answered depended on my biased opinion of other chocolate companies with a lot of condensed analysis thrown in.

Jeff de Bruges's shop concept is visually stunning and instantly recognizable as being their brand. As Neuhaus's secondary line, Jeff de Bruges's chocolate is exceptional. Molds are used across both brands, and certain recipes cross over, making Jeff de Bruges's quality better than to be expected for the price. I had shopped about ten Jeff de Bruges stores over a year before I was able to think of anything our salespeople could say when asked about them.

The first chocolate store I visit in certain European cities will be Jeff de Bruges's because I have favorite pieces I must stock up on, particularly their foil wrapped mint. But therein lies the problem: Jeff de Bruges does not offer every one of their chocolate pieces throughout the year. Godiva would never do that and leave customers disappointed. Godiva's comeback to customers comparing us to Jeff de Bruges became, "Well, it's phenomenal if they have what you want."

Corné Port-Royal makes my favorite vanilla truffle. I suspect it might be made with Madagascar vanilla beans somehow steeped in vanilla ganache. Truffles have a ganache center. Godiva stores downplayed them as Corné Port-Royal's "buttercreams," a subtle dig, because a buttercream is not as rich, decadent, and full-flavored as a truffle.

What was once a staid brand, Mary had come out of hibernation and vaulted into the upper pantheons of luxury chocolate retailers during the 1990s. "Domino" (dark caramel) is my favorite chocolate from Mary. But Mary stores appear committed to the traditional looks of the 1960s and Mary packaging reflects that. At Godiva we used to say, "Mary can't match Godiva's selection of cute seasonal boxes."

If you can't find Belgian chocolates, the next best thing are Swiss chocolates. Teuscher from Zurich franchises worldwide, so at Godiva we reacted to them by saying, "They're a *franchise*." Upon entering a Teuscher store, once you overlook the unique store décor and packaging, Teuscher's champagne truffles truly are worth $120 per pound.

At the other end of the spectrum is a popularly-priced company from California. See's is the one brand on Earth that could take over. See's could be number one in sales worldwide in a heartbeat if they wanted to. Sees' business model is every chocolatier's dream. See's enjoys strong brand recognition, industry-leading customer loyalty retention, and See's stores deliver sales per square foot which are rumored in the industry to be higher than Godiva's.

For someone who has not been to See's to understand their chocolate, I would best describe See's as home-made style, honest confectionery made with quality ingredients. See's cares about what they do. The price though has jumped from $17.50 a pound before the pandemic to $32 per pound after.

See's was a sleeping giant whose only expansion had been during the fourth quarter annually into temporary pop-up kiosks at malls across the US. But then See's opened in Macau, and people wondered if that was the beginning of See's global takeover. The only thing we could say about See's at Godiva was, "They make customers do all the work," because the line at See's stretches out the door while customers pick their own chocolates to pack each box. The point of Godiva was for chocolates to be packed in the boxes at the factory, so the decorative ribbons, bows, and adornments could be tied on there, prior to shipping. All Godiva store personnel needed to do upon receipt was unpack the boxes and sell them.

Having embarked on store expansion with a business plan, and navigated around competitors, I next had to learn how to package Godiva. What was Godiva going to be? Since Godiva was sold in fashion malls and at fashion department stores, it made sense to position Godiva as a fashion brand. A decision was made never to repeat a seasonal packaging collection. Each year's packaging, be it for Easter, Valentine's, or Christmas, would be new and collectible. A theme was created for each season, such as "Springtime in Brussels" for Easter and "The Glory of Giving" for Christmas.

As Godiva pricing increased over time, I noticed consumers who could no longer afford a one-pound box simply traded down to a half-pound box. Customers were managing their average check, which is preferable to having customers manage their number of visits. Godiva advertising continued to attract a bigger pool of customers in total. Godiva sales increased to $250 million per year in the US alone by the end of the 1990s. Godiva marketing reinforced the "want" because no one "needs" gourmet chocolate.

Chapter 3

OVERHAULING GODIVA

To increase sales by $100 million, I needed Godiva's entire approach to marketing to be overhauled. But there was a problem: I had to sway the consensus of an entire organization of colleagues who basically did not sense that there was anything that needed to be overhauled.

Prior to my arrival, Godiva marketing had been focused on food attributes, such as flavors and tastes and elegance as a dessert presentation. But, I decided, there was only so much product Godiva could sell as long as chocolate was merely considered something to eat. My goal was to expand our playing field to be able to compete in categories besides confectionery. We were spending millions designing packaging, so it made sense to me that Godiva should be marketed as a gift. People buying a gift box to give someone else would not be eating the contents themselves. The focus of Godiva's ad campaigns had to shift *to* appealing to shoppers seeking alternatives to other gift categories and *away* from merely describing new "seasonal flavors."

Does sales lead marketing, or does marketing lead sales? The marketing department's annual budget for advertising was $10 million per year. Designing campaigns and placing ads was not the challenge. My issue was how to completely change the way of thinking in the sales department. Plus, I hadn't yet put my finger on which way to steer the ship. Where would Godiva's new market positioning lead the brand?

Because our primary sales channel was department stores, my first instinct was to emphasize bold packaging to create the persona of Godiva being an upscale fashion product. However, to make a decision about what the future might hold if I wanted Godiva to be perceived as being less about chocolate and more as "something else," I needed to get more data from Godiva's sales force.

Without telling anyone my plan, I attended the annual convention of Godiva sales representatives. This decision would turn out to be fortuitous, because having everyone who calls on customers in a room provided me with a "one-stop shopping" opportunity to pick their brains. I needed to know what the buyers were saying during sales meetings. Listening for a thru-line about what takes place in those conversations could provide the clue I was looking for regarding Godiva's new direction.

Godiva's stylish and all female sales force met in Phoenix. Godiva's wholesale sales team consisted of twelve account executives. Each account executive managed a geographic territory of the US representing about $10 million in annual sales. Account executives worked from home and looked forward to getaway travels. For this meeting, held at the Boulders Resort, everyone got to stay in their own "casita" set on landscaped grounds amongst pools, tennis courts, and golf courses.

Their reason for this trip was to participate in a chocolate tasting ceremony. The marketing department's goal was to decide which new flavors of chocolates to test in stores for Mother's Day. Godiva had a very specific set of protocols for this annual tradition, which was significant because "limited edition" Mother's Day chocolates that sold well became a permanent part of Godiva's year-round lineup.

In attendance was Vivianna, the young college graduate from Los Angeles. Vivianna had landed the job because her father was president of Robinson's, our largest US account at the time. Sitting next to Vivianna was Brielle, the parking garage queen from San Francisco. Brielle's father had bet on building parking garages after World War II and left them to her when he died. Brielle did not need to work but considered Godiva to be "light housekeeping," and it gave her something to do. Brandy from Miami was seated next to Brielle. Across the table was Caliope, the loudmouth from Atlanta who considered herself to be the alpha female. Caliope really did get the job done, even if it meant boozing and cruising with the buyers to get a purchase order (PO). Sitting two seats down from Caliope was the dedicated lifer, Mary-Margaret from Philadelphia. Mary-Margaret had been the chocolate buyer at Wanamaker's, and we rescued her when Wanamaker's went out of business. At the head of the table was Lacey from New York, the firebrand intellectual who genuinely put in a full day's work.

The group met in the high-ceilinged, elegantly appointed clubhouse around an enormous conference table, seated in upholstered armchairs on casters. On the table, ten gold platters were arranged, each holding one new type of chocolate. The chocolates were lined up like soldiers in precise rows several layers high, creating a pyramid. The room had an overhead projector beaming images onto a huge screen that dropped down from the ceiling. Bottles of Evian water were set at each place along with small china plates and white cloth napkins.

The creative force behind Godiva's recipe development was the master chocolatier, Barrett, who had flown to Arizona from Pennsylvania. Each year Barrett created new chocolate flavors in unique shapes for the sales force to taste. The secret fillings of Barrett's truffles were revealed during these ceremonies, as the samples (which had never been seen outside his chocolate laboratory) were unveiled to the sales team.

Barrett seemed out of place at Godiva. He was quite cerebral and extremely well-educated. Barrett had nothing in common with any of the women in sales. They travelled the country on lavish expense accounts, while Barrett clocked in every day at a grey industrial warehouse in the suburbs of Philadelphia. Barrett's work was also highly secretive, causing him to be hesitant when answering questions as if the salespeople were trying to pry sensitive information from him. Barrett's reserved personality was the opposite of the gregarious sales team's high energy.

Picture my elite squad of chocolate power brokers gathered around the conference table. The procedure was that as each prototype chocolate sample was described, the sales force could debate their no-holds-barred opinion of whether each truffle had what it takes to deserve the honor of being named, marketed, photographed, then splashed across billboards and bus stops around the country.

The festivities began after lunch when Barrett's colleague Anitra, from marketing, handed out something resembling a dessert menu. Printed in gold leaf on parchment card stock was a chocolate spec sheet, containing ingredient information and an allergy declaration pertaining to each masterpiece Barrett had laid out on the table.

The tasting ceremony was choreographed with precision. As the lights dimmed in the room, a photo appeared on the overhead screen, and Barrett began introducing the first chocolate up for consideration that day.

"Meet Godiva's new Blackberry Truffle, a decadent 71 percent dark single-origin Peru ganache with crystalized blackberry crumbles, enrobed in dark chocolate and garnished with dried blackberry pieces," Barrett effused to a round of applause as pictures were snapped.

Anitra continued, "This flavor profile fills a need for fruity centers, which are trending, and blackberry complements our top-ten selling raspberry truffle."

Anitra gestured to the beckoning tray of truffles, saying, "Now give us your opinion!"

As the tray was passed around the table, picture the exquisitely dressed women of Godiva, who had a powerful feminine way of presenting themselves (think "Pamela Anderson goes to court"). With expensive haircuts, perfect nails, real jewelry, whitened teeth, and accessories out of the pages of a fashion magazine, most had a personal trainer, and the ladies were almost always on a diet. Few ate candy.

"No, thank you," Vivianna said, while her eyes widened, as if she was longing to reach out and grab one before passing the tray to Brielle.

"These look divine. Great job, Barrett," Brielle proclaimed as she gave the tray a respectable look before passing it on.

The rest of the women repeated this reaction, continuing around the table with the tray untouched until it got to Caliope, sitting third from the end. Caliope took two. She popped one in her mouth, but not before saying, "One for later," setting a Blackberry Truffle on her plate.

As Caliope passed the tray of samples down to the last two women, who also politely declined a taste, Mary-Margaret was just about ready to set the tray back down in the middle of the table when Caliope spoke up.

"Oh, um... here, let me help you, Mary-Margaret. There's room right here in front of me," Caliope said, which of course made no sense because there was room to set the tray down anywhere.

This was met with completely non-plussed blank stares emanating from the faces of the other women as Mary-Margaret passed the tray right back down to Caliope, who proceeded to take two more blackberry chocolates and put them on her plate. Then she set the tray down.

Anitra and Barrett were not annoyed that nobody wanted to taste their new chocolate creations. Like fine wine, chocolate is a product that people do not have to consume in order to assess whether the product will sell. While the purpose of the meeting was ostensibly to get everybody's opinion, Anitra wanted to empower her staff back in Philly to decide; after all, she was the one who told Barrett what to make in the first place.

Barrett knew how the game was played. Account executives called on retail buyers who couldn't care less which pieces were in the boxes. Buyers want to talk numbers—what is the cost, what is the retail price, what are the margins? Buyers worked in office buildings at headquarters, not in the branch stores, and would never see the chocolates, let alone taste them. But the account executives had to at least know some of the names of the chocolates in case anyone were ever to ask.

"What does everybody think?" Barrett asked.

The women had a lot to say. Laptops were pulled up, sales figures were discussed, product rankings were reviewed, and there was no shortage of opinions as to whether blackberry was a classic flavor people craved. The final consensus was summed up by Lacey, who said, "strawberry would be better."

Barrett moved on to the next new flavor as the group settled in for a few hours of chocolate talk.

Caliope knew how the game was played, too! Once each tray was passed around, if there were extra chocolates left, whoever wanted more could have some. Caliope never met a chocolate she didn't like. As the meeting progressed throughout the afternoon, Caliope ate six pieces, and Anitra gave Caliope a to-go box to hold all the samples accumulated on Caliope's plate. The clock struck 2:00; the clock struck 3:00 as Caliope led the debate about the new flavors while Barrett and Anitra took notes.

Finally, the time came for a vote, and four of the ten new pieces received the required two-thirds vote from the sales force to move on to Mother's Day testing. Blackberry Truffles did not make the cut.

Just when everybody thought the meeting was about to adjourn in time to get in a round of golf or hit the pool, two servers from the Boulders came in to refresh the water and coffee. "Come here and give us your opinions," Caliope beckoned, offering them a choice from the personal stash she had collected. One tried a Birthday Cake, and the other sampled a Chocolate Chip Cookie Dough.

There is one troublemaker in every company. Caliope deviated from the script by asking the opinions of random people who were not necessarily part of Godiva's target demographic (college-educated, well-traveled, over $100,000 per year in household income, repeat customer). What was happening in Phoenix that day was that the real chocolate-lover of the group lost sight of the fact that the kind of chocolate Godiva made didn't matter. Whatever Godiva put its name on sold.

"What do you think?" Caliope asked.

"I like Russell Stover's better," the woman responded.

"I prefer Whitman's," the gentleman stated.

That was certainly not the response you want to hear in a room full of Godiva salespeople!

The meeting had taken a turn because an unwritten rule of Godiva was broken, that being the only opinions about chocolates which ultimately mattered were those of the gatekeepers, department store buyers who had the power of the pen to place million-dollar orders. The battle fought by Godiva every season was against other chocolate brands for a bigger share of the budget from retailers including Marshall Field and Lord & Taylor. The battle was won when the retailer's wire transfer came through for payment. There was never a bigger war for shelf space going on in retailers' stores because once each chain received their shipments, they had already bought the product, owned it, and had to sell it. Department stores created monumental chocolate displays using temporary fixturing on every floor. I liked to tell analysts that Godiva created shelf space where none had existed before.

Consumers, upon seeing these shrines to Godiva on the selling floor at their favorite retailer, quickly gave in to temptation and made an impulse buy based on factors such as Godiva's reputation, and the surroundings adjacent to other shiny bright merchandise such as jewelry, cosmetics, handbags, and shoes. The public bought Godiva as an aspirational purchase. Everyone wanted to live the Godiva lifestyle.

Feedback that filtered up from account executives talking about their meetings with retail chain buyers revealed that Godiva actually competed as a gift against perfume, flowers, and champagne. Brandy mentioned Bloomingdales' spring promotion displaying Godiva in the fragrances department. Lacey told the group about the way Wegman's sold Godiva and champagne on the same endcap. Brielle explained that Bristol Farms featured Godiva in their floral department at the front of each store near the cash registers. Vivianna revealed that during Christmas planning meetings, Robinsons had decided Godiva would move to the picture frame department because those were Robinsons' two best-selling Christmas gift categories.

Godiva's operating paradigm was reset after these discussions in Phoenix. We as a group decided that too much emphasis was being put on the chocolates when the public thought of us more as a gift and less as a food. Not enough focus was being made on the packaging we put our chocolates in.

In Phoenix, we set out to make the Godiva gold ballotin become iconic. My goal was to make the purchase decision at retail be about the gift presentation, taking the emphasis off which chocolates were in the box. Seasonal collections simply became the gold ballotin with some type of collectible decoration tied around the bow. We sold the gold ballotin in popular sizes, from a quarter-pound up to a three-pound box. The gold ballotin would go on to become synonymous with the Godiva brand; they were one and the same.

The Phoenix conclave was the beginning of establishing the Godiva the world knows today, a marketing company. Godiva was able to gain mass market share on the mid- to high-end by offering an elegant gold box packed with a vaguely familiar assortment of chocolates inside. We never really changed the chocolates again.

The same thirty-two pieces were to be found in Godiva's one pound box for the next twenty years. As a side benefit, training in the stores was simplified to sales associates using one line, "This is *Godiva*," implying that people were expected to know what that meant.

Within five years after this meeting took place, Godiva had officially become a seasonal gifting business as measured by the numbers. June, July, and August sales combined accounted for less than 2 percent of annual sales because there are no gifting holidays during summer. But the last ten days before Christmas accounted for over 60 percent of sales. It was all about the presentation; packaging is everything.

Chapter 4

A WALK IN THE PARK

Godiva rented out the Brussels Opera House for one of our annual conventions. Every other year, the entire organization's employees attended Godiva conventions in rotating cities. That meant, during those alternating years, Godiva's convention was a large meeting, with people flying in from all over the world. Retail store managers and wholesale field sales executives working on every continent, joined headquarters staff and both factory teams for the assembly. Godiva employed staff working in the duty-free division, the traffic department, ingredient sourcing, accounting, labeling compliance, and all of the other careers that needed to synergize in order for Godiva to be Godiva. For us to accommodate a gathering of over five hundred employees, we needed a large venue, centrally located. Brussels Opera House provided just the dramatic backdrop needed that year.

But make no mistake, everyone attending knew that the purpose of this confab was for the packaging team to take the reins and lead the charge during formal meetings. Break-out functions during the day, introduced upcoming packaging collections, which would be workshopped according to launch plans for each continent. From an artistic standpoint, each of these sessions were "a study," representing the final chance for the packaging development team to make changes to the packaging before ordering containers of it to fill with chocolates for sale.

Sheer geniuses ran the art department. My lifelong takeaway from having worked at Godiva was the happiness that comes from being surrounded by unsurpassed brilliance. I love smart people. There is a popular belief that "left-brain/right-brain" circuitry prevents artists from being business people. I did not see that to be the case at Godiva. It was magical the way Godiva's in-house artists could sketch a collection, hand-make sample boxes, and do so all while keeping in mind the commercial goal of their seasonal packaging line. Somehow our artists knew which designs would sell. I asked Cathy, the head of the department, how this type of talent came to be. She explained that her master's degree was in color theory (which I never knew existed), and that each artist collaborating on a project had a unique specialty, such as proportions and measurements, even custom font design! I was not aware that Godiva employed full-time people who did nothing but invent new fonts for each packaging collection.

Each artist on Godiva's team rotated responsibility for taking a leadership position designing whatever collection was coming up next. The seasons ran: fall, Halloween, Thanksgiving, Hanukah, Christmas, Lunar New Year, Valentine's, White Day, Easter, Mother's Day, Father's Day, and Fourth of July/Bastille Day. Based on the date when the convention was held, several season's worth of packaging might be "revealed" to the global team, depending on how many collections were ready to go. This was not a "sneak peek," it was a full-on assault, bombarding primarily the sales team with ammunition to understand the motivation behind whatever theme had been chosen. The more salespeople understood design concepts, the better they could sell.

Sometimes, artists partnered up with each other to design a theme, or switched the order around, to enable artists to work on a holiday they felt personally connected with or motivated to work on due to a design inspiration. Rest assured that every effort put forth was designed with selling chocolate in mind. Consumer packaged goods must resonate with shoppers in such a way that the display physically—literally—"stops traffic" in stores. Customers needed to feel the Godiva boxes were "pretty," which meant *giftable,* and no one knew that more than the artists who were reviewed on the performance of their collections. Good designs meant raises and promotions; bad designs meant taking a break from working as a lead designer, or worse yet, being sent back to the branches to spend a year working as a store manager to learn what the public truly expects to see when they walk into a mall.

I was expecting to see some sort of bombshell being dropped on the entire organization when Cathy called to notify me as a heads-up that she was personally going to make the annual fall packaging presentation at the Brussels Opera House (but I didn't know what the bombshell would be). It was highly unusual for a senior executive vice president to design a grouping as opposed to overseeing a staff who designed the grouping, and signing off on their design. Cathy told me she reserved a front-row seat for me, so I should ask the ushers to escort me in, and that part of her dramatic build-up would be to keep everyone waiting until the audience saw I was seated, at which point she would begin (so I should arrive precisely one minute before 6:00 p.m.).

"I'm taking a page from your book," Cathy stated directly and with no ambiguity. She went on to say, "The entire packaging team has spent months orchestrating an entirely new way to give Godiva's product line the impact it deserves in front of the firm's worldwide executives." In other words, Cathy was throwing down the gauntlet! She was saying that this was her way of advocating for the packaging design department. Packaging wanted the white-hot-shining-spotlight, and boy were they about to get it!

The closing gala black-tie dinner on the final night of the convention would be catered in the cavernous lobby of the Opera House. Cathy's presentation would occur just before the pre-dinner cocktail hour. I arrived as directed, wearing a Thierry Mugler opalescent pearlized metallic black tuxedo, taking my orchestra row seat, as the auditorium lights dimmed, with a packed house of people not knowing that tonight would be more than just a typical sales presentation. Cathy saw me and signaled from the wings, waving ever so slightly, that it was "go" time.

Cathy stepped out from the wings, spotlighted, and as she did, the conductor started up the orchestra. I had not expected the entire forty-four-piece Brussels Philharmonic would be providing accompaniment. Something unexpected happened: a slide show began. A cavernous movie screen had been silently dropping down from the ceiling above the stage behind Cathy. On the screen were images of chestnuts, chipmunks, acorns, and fall leaves blowing through a park.

Cathy spoke into the microphone with all the confidence of a person who had lived a thousand lives. She spoke in conjunction with what the images behind her conveyed, but without ever having to turn around to look. Cathy just *knew* about her subject. Come back with me to that night, and hear what Cathy said:

"As I enjoyed the last days of summer, under a bright sun and a beautiful sky, how could I not help but feeling like taking *a walk in the park*. The scene was familiar and comforting, helping remind me that the changing of the seasons is the way of life for people, plants, and animals. The leaves on the trees were starting to change colors from green to brown, and as they did, a gentle breeze pushed some leaves off the trees, and they fluttered by me as the leaves fell towards the ground. The chipmunks in the hedges gathered acorns in their cheeks as they could sense the change in seasons. Flocks of birds overhead knew that it was fall in the park as they started flying south for winter. Children played in the grass, people read books on park benches, and I explored the pathways through the flowers as I took *a walk in the park*."

Suddenly the symphony stopped. Fall images on the movie screen transitioned into printed words appearing that read, "A Walk in the Park."

"Meet Godiva's fall collection, 'A Walk in the Park,'" Cathy announced, and then multi-colored orange, green, and brown fall-colored spotlights started popping across the stage like orbs. The audience applauded.

One by one, slides began beaming images of each box in Godiva's newly designed fall collection. The philharmonic played "September" in the background (a pop song with lyrics by Earth, Wind, and Fire) while Cathy introduced her one-pound box, her half-pound box, her quarter-pound box, and then, the designs for all-new fall gifts, including a box of all milk chocolates shaped like leaves and a box of all dark chocolates shaped like acorns. The ribbons were printed to say, "A Walk in the Park." And hanging from each bow was a decorative keepsake collectible keychain shaped like an acorn or a leaf.

I didn't see that coming! Godiva had never added adornments to the packaging previously. For a moment I experienced déja-vu, making me wonder if I had ESP and was seeing success about to manifest. I knew this was what we had been looking for.

Suddenly the orchestra reached a denouement as Cathy passionately continued describing her excitement about how easy it would be for the sales team to sell this fall collection to department stores, and the spotlight on her grew and grew in size and intensity, her voice becoming louder with each sentence. Cathy stepped out from behind the podium, walking to stage right, walking to stage left, gesturing to the screen, talking about acorns, leaves, and chipmunks like a crazed person as if the only subject that mattered on earth was the fall coloration of Godiva boxes and the perfect width of Godiva ribbons.

The audience's excitement was palpable. There was an energy I had never sensed before. Even the Opera House staff had stopped what they were doing to gaze intently at the stage.

The orchestra pit rose. The stage lit up like Shea Stadium for a night game. The decibel level intensified as the philharmonic's cadence matched Cathy's footsteps. Giant numbers dropped down into view from above stage like you'd see on the bonus round of a TV game show. Cathy shouted—screamed—hollered—at the audience like it was a Sunday church revival: "I give you Godiva's first $10 million fall collection!" The audience roared, everyone was on their feet, there was a standing ovation, the house lights came up, the numbers sparkled like they were glittered, and the band played, "The Battle Hymn of the Republic." Two tables on wheels were pushed out from the left and right sides of the stage. Both tables displayed examples of the actual boxes. Cathy held her arms out wide, tilted her head back, looked up at the ceiling, and repeated the name so nobody could ever forget it: "A WALK IN THE PARK!" Cathy started taking her bows! She bowed straight ahead; she walked stage right and took a bow; she walked stage left and took a bow; she came back to center stage, took a bow, and as she was bent over, looked me right in the eye and winked. Cathy had known what she was doing all along. This was planned.

Cathy was ushering in a brand-new day. Godiva was going to start assigning sales goals to the sales force. That was something I had never done before. In the past, I used to wait for orders to come in. I'd just "see what happened" and "wait to see how it sold." After Cathy's pronouncement, the sales team had a number to hit. The sales force was ecstatic because if they had $10 million worth of chocolate inventory to sell, they'd earn commissions on $10 million!

Cathy was triumphant. I went to see her back-stage as the audience filtered out of the auditorium for cocktail hour in the lobby. "I bet you weren't expecting a multi-media performance, were you?" Cathy asked.

"Congratulations, Cathy!" I boomed as I shook hands with all of her department's staff, who had gathered around the "A Walk in the Park" samples. "Something tells me you rehearsed that!"

I picked up a box and scrutinized the pattern closely. Once I was sure, I said, "Cathy, I think that's a squirrel, not a chipmunk."

She put her glasses on and stared intently at the box, letting the spotlight illuminate the design clearly. "No, that's definitely a chipmunk. I should know; I designed him!" Cathy replied.

"But squirrels have big fluffy tails like that, and chipmunks have an overbite," I protested.

Exasperated, Cathy let out a roar, "*Celine*!" (calling out for her assistant), looking around.

I just left them to ponder that thought. I always had to have the final say.

Cathy and I were seated next to each other at the dinner that night. When Cathy and I spoke that evening, she went on to explain, "My point was to get everybody to realize why the fall collection will be so easy for customers to understand. Sometimes we have to stick with the basics, designing a subject matter everyone can relate to."

This convention was where Godiva's "gift with purchase" idea came from. Godiva's "signature look" during my era will be remembered for having Godiva boxes feature some type of tiny ornaments tied around the bows. It never ceases to amaze me how many people's memories are of saving and collecting these treasures long after the chocolate was eaten. People remember where they were in life when someone presented them with a box of Godiva, and they saved the ornament from that period as a memento all these years later (which now is over twenty years ago).

Initial sales were OK but nowhere near great. Many of the "A Walk in the Park" boxes were printed cardboard featuring fall images drawn by Cathy. I knew we had to find a way to build off the momentum from the Phoenix conclave when it became apparent that the public expects Godiva to be sold in the gold ballotin. It seemed when our chocolate wasn't presented in a ballotin, it wasn't Godiva to a lot of people.

"A Walk in the Park" sold about $2 million in each of the Asian, European, and North American territories. "A Walk in the Park" ribbon, specific to the fall season, provided a clue. It was the ribbon that provided three-dimensional "pop" and resonated in the public's mind with "fall." Plus, Cathy's team had ordered plain white cardboard "collars" to wrap around each ribbon when the factory packed boxes in cartons for shipping, to avoid the ribbons being crushed. So much care and attention had been given to the custom ribbon that I wanted to explore that angle.

The gold ballotin was Godiva's signature slope-sided box. Since Godiva's inception, ballotins had always been tied with the matching gold string that was manufactured by the vendor providing the ballotins. I decided to capitalize on the iconic status of Godiva's basic ballotin by adorning the ballotins seasonally. I started replacing the gold string with seasonal ribbon. The distinction was far from subtle!

Dangling from the ribbon, we tied miniature ornaments, and those became instant collectibles. Tying ornaments from Godiva *ribboned* ballotins became the solution for iconic packaging that would be instantly recognizable on a consistent basis from season to season. The ribbons would change, never the ballotin. That did it! It was the contrast of thick, luxurious ribbons against the gold filigree metallic ballotin, offset with a dangling keepsake, that became Godiva's "look."

How many readers still have the tiny wooden cello and gold metal horn Christmas tree ornaments in their collections of holiday décor? Those came from late-1980's "Symphony of Christmas" collection when our ballotins featured blue ribbons with small musical instruments dangling from the bow as an homage to an orchestra playing Christmas carols.

In 1997's Valentine's Day line, "Sweets for the Sweet," featured red heart ribbons tied around the ballotins with heart-shaped cameo picture frames attached. In 1998's Easter collection, "Here Comes Peter Cottontail," ballotins had green ribbons with Easter bunny key chains tied around them.

I came up with those names for each seasonal theme, so Godiva's sales reps could go into meetings at department store buying offices and introduce a "collection" by name rather than just saying, "Here is our Thanksgiving packaging." It helped sell because buyers innately understood each collection was a one-time buy with no re-ordering possible. Around this time, I also instituted the "non-cancelable" clause in Godiva's terms and conditions. This resulted in orders coming in earlier, "while quantities were available," and in bigger quantities; if a seasonal collection were to sell out far before a holiday, the only back-up chocolate available to fill fixturing would be in plain gold ballotins with gold string.

For Mother's Day, the ribbon and the small greeting card attached both depicted flowers on a trellis, so I called it, "Through the Garden Gate." A Christmas collection's ribbon depicting Harlequin jesters was named "The Life of the Party" and had a bottle opener as the ornament. Halloween was "Frightful Night." We never ran out of ideas, even going so far as naming one Lunar New Year grouping, "The Year of the Rabbit," for which the factory produced bite-sized rabbit-shaped white chocolate caramels to pack in the ballotins.

Sales records were broken. The year Godiva was first Koshered, we introduced "Happy Hanukah" in all markets worldwide and sold an incremental $1 million in Hanukah packaging. I believed "Happy Hanukah's" sales were purely incremental because all Godiva was Kosher, not just that year's "Happy Hanukah" grouping. At first, not everyone at Godiva saw that distinction. In other words, would Godiva have sold another million dollars' worth of chocolate at Hanukah if we had not offered the specific collection?

There was always a four-dollar price difference at retail once this initiative became Godiva's permanent way of doing business.

Customers could still choose to buy the plain gold ballotin with the basic gold string in our boutiques. For four dollars more, customers could opt for the decorated ballotin with the keepsake ornament. Godiva margin goals had to be maintained. The jangling add-ons and fancy ribbons cost money.

The factory only shipped empty plain gold ballotins and matching gold string for hand-packing in Godiva boutiques. That encouraged more customers to buy pre-packs if they wanted the décor. This resulted in measurable labor savings. We had always sought ways to discourage people from wanting to select their own assortment of thirty-two pieces of chocolate to fill a custom ballotin. Salespeople could now simply explain, "Decorated ballotins come from the factory already ribboned. We don't have the ribbon or the picks to add to ballotins here at the store."

Retail chains typically ordered a fifty-fifty ratio of plain gold ballotins to decorated gold ballotins in all sizes. What I found interesting was that reports came back saying the decorated ballotins sold out first. As I suspected, there was no price resistance among Godiva customers.

I soon ran a contest. Winning retail partners would receive an enormous gold ballotin "prop" for display, measuring about two feet across. It was designed to hang above the Godiva counter as a visual way of attracting attention. The winners were based on which department store had the highest sales increase, but in reality, I ordered one "prop" for each account executive and left it up to them to decide who the winner was going to be in their regions. Imagine my surprise one day when I was touring a mall in Tulsa, Oklahoma and a store there of all places had a winning prop on display! I later found out that whenever I announced visits to branches, stores were "dressed up" to look their best. I never knew that was happening! No wonder I kept seeing two-foot-long Godiva ballotins all across the country, more than I had ever ordered—they were being moved around constantly.

Over the last few decades, as I have followed Godiva, I have been watching to see what each subsequent leader's "stamp" on the brand would be. I have not really noticed any individual after me having a substantial impact on Godiva's brand appearance, competitive positioning, or store operations. What does that say? Upon meeting some of Godiva's more recent executives at trade shows and industry conferences, they all said versions of the same thing: that what they were trying to do could not be aligned with what they were actually able to accomplish. Their spin was that Godiva's shareholders have become much more conservative over the years. I think other people prefer taking on far more administrative roles than had been my hands-on approach.

Chapter 5

WOULD YOU LIKE A SAMPLE?

Godiva's test store was in Altamonte Mall in Seminole County, the wealthy northern suburbs of Orlando. The store was located on the first floor, center court, between Robinson's and Burdines.

Many Fortune 500s used Orlando area locations to test new menu items and consumer packaged goods because a broad cross-section of tourists from all over the country visited Central Florida.

At the time, Altamonte's top-line gross sales were $250,000 per year. Compare that to Century City in Los Angeles, which grossed $25,000 per day during the last ten days before Christmas. In ten days, Century City took in $250,000 in sales, the same volume as Altamonte sold in a year.

We put up with the relatively low sales figures at Altamonte because the boutique was an idea laboratory. The location had a typical general manager, Mark, who fit Godiva's profile of presentable men who could talk to women and sell chocolate. Since all Godiva shops were corporately owned, that made Mark a career

W-2 employee who should have been familiar with Godiva's corporate culture, including policies and procedures.

I visited Mark in May 1987 to see where he planned to install the new ice cream scooping cabinet since Godiva was preparing to launch ice cream. We would sell ice cream cones and ice cream sundaes with hot fudge and chocolate sprinkles. A major remodel would have to happen in time for summer.

When we entered the stockroom to see where the upright freezer to store ice cream deliveries would go, I noticed something strange. There were pallets all over the storage room floor with unopened cases of pre-packed chocolates stacked on top of them.

"Where is your back-room refrigerator?" I asked.

Mark replied, "This store doesn't have one."

"All the other stores do," I responded, knowing this was a brand standard. "Why don't you surprise me?" I told him, hinting that Mark should coordinate installing a backroom refrigerator when the contractor remodeled his store for ice cream.

Mark of all people knew he had access to unlimited funds from the real estate department's budget because at Godiva, money was never an issue. Making room was not an issue either because wasted space was taken up by a manager's desk, piled high with *Sports Illustrated* magazines. Mark said he would come up with an ice cream menu for the summer, and I left.

That fall I returned to Altamonte. I was standing in the mall, looking at the remodeled store through the picture windows. Seeing me, Mark ran up excitedly and exclaimed, "I've got a surprise to show you!"

Literally guiding me back to the employee service area, Mark pushed open the stock room door and announced, "I got a refrigerated stockroom!"

I scanned to the left, scanned to the right, and looked straight ahead, but all I saw was an ordinary home refrigerator like the ones sold at Sears in the very same mall.

This can't be happening, I remember thinking. We entered, and I walked up to the white, two-door refrigerator, which was surrounded on both sides with pallets of chocolate cartons now stacked to the ceiling! The point of having a walk-in refrigerator would be to put the chocolate in the refrigerator, not on the ground next to the refrigerator. Astonished, all I could say was, "I just have to peek inside," as I opened the refrigerator door. The only thing inside was a few employee lunches! To this day I still cannot imagine what Mark was thinking. He was so proud of himself, too. This was truly a rare circumstance when I was speechless because the situation was so unfathomable. Since ice cream turned out to be the biggest disaster in Godiva history, I closed Altamonte when the lease was up.

(Fashionably dressed women tapping their high heels impatiently while being kept waiting to buy forty-five-dollar boxes of chocolate as the staff served teenagers three-dollar ice cream cones that dripped all over the floor was not a successful test. And for the record, it was not my idea in the first place.)

I needed to transfer Mark somewhere besides another store. In 1988 a new pilot program was budgeted to launch. Mark was put in charge of developing that program, which requires some background explanation.

I had been seeking an explosive marketing idea to push sales from the bottom-up. There used to be a term, "guerilla marketing," referring to field marketing done at the local level. That was what I wanted to accomplish, pushing marketing down to the point of purchase but done in a way to further differentiate Godiva from competitors. Competitors were not offering samples.

The term for this Godiva program was "demoing." A "demo" referred to handing out free chocolate samples in front of the Godiva counter. My theory was that once a person tasted our chocolate, they would make an impulse decision to buy some Godiva on the spot. Having demonstrators standing in the aisles provided an opportunity to stop customers in their tracks and get them to consider whether they might need a gift purchase while at the mall that day.

The first detail to address was the cost of giving away Godiva chocolates. First of all, each piece was too expensive to just give away. Second of all, I couldn't have demonstrators taking chocolate out of the case to give away because we needed to maintain inventory control. There would have to be a special type of chocolates created as giveaways for the demo program. Stores would not ordinarily sell the pieces of chocolate being "demoed."

That is where Mark came back into the picture. I put Mark in charge of Godiva's new demo program. He worked with the factory in Pennsylvania to produce thin squares of solid chocolate called *demitasse* chocolate. I was quite happy with Mark's solution because a small box of demitasse squares contained over five hundred pieces of giveaway chocolates. These sampling pieces were very inexpensive to produce and a couple of boxes per store would last four hours based on typical foot traffic.

People will be astonished to learn the actual dollar amount Godiva spent on giving away samples. It was going to cost a half-million-dollars per year to mount a national demo campaign. Godiva's sales were a half-million-dollars per day, meaning the annual expenditure for demos represented about a day's sales. That was a gamble I could take. But mounting a demo campaign was easier said than done.

Manufacturing small chocolate demitasse squares to hand out as tasting bites was no problem—Godiva manufactured 70,000 pounds an hour. That translates into making enough chocolate to fill a twenty-foot container every forty-five minutes. As a matter of fact, 90 percent of the half-million-dollar annual sampling budget was spent on paying the people who handed out samples in stores that sold Godiva.

Godiva's terminology was to call this army of seasonal helpers, "demonstrators." Dependable demonstrators who worked season after season for many years might be called upon to also serve as "rotators." Rotators drove around to stores in their district to check the date codes. Both classifications of on-call, part-time brand ambassadors were hired through employment agencies and paid as freelance independent contractors.

However, there was no such thing as a temp agency specializing in retail folks who worked four-hour shifts every Saturday afternoon during the months of December, February, and April. Godiva first needed to identify alternative, highly-specialized agencies in big cities that hired "spritzers." ("Spritzers" was the term for manufacturer's representatives who stand in the fragrance department spraying perfume or cologne, so shoppers could smell the newest celebrity scent.) I would get the owners of spritzing agencies on the phone and say we wanted the agency to branch out into chocolate. My pitch would make it sound so easy: all the agencies had to do was schedule their roster of spritzers to give out samples on days we needed them. Spritzers were already accustomed to driving to the malls in town. They knew who the store managers were and where the stockrooms were. Plus, Godiva overpaid to such an extent that it was ridiculous. That meant no agency ever said "no."

Little did the people running these agencies know what they were getting themselves into. Managing hundreds of demonstrators was like herding cats. People had to wear a Godiva apron, they had to show up, they had to know something about chocolate to be able to sell, and they had to fill out paperwork to get paid. The paperwork sent demonstrators over the edge because people who liked talking to the public and gossiping about retailing and chocolate for four hours were not the type of personalities who wanted to have to take a count, keep track of sales that day, or check for expired date codes. It was only a matter of time before any agency would resign the Godiva account—typically after about one season to be exact!

That all changed when I got a phone call from Liza Bamberger in Bradenton. Liza had gone on maternity leave. She wanted to remain associated with Godiva but did not want to work full-time after having her baby. Liza was a problem solver and gave me the best idea I had heard in a long time. She wanted to form a national demo agency. In cities where she had friends and relatives, Liza and her team would directly recruit, train, schedule, and supervise demonstrators. In other cities, she would sub-contract to local agencies that would follow her best practices to the letter, in order to develop a long-term, consistent and dependable stable of national demonstrators. It was almost as if Liza was suggesting starting a franchise of demo agencies. Liza told me the name she had chosen: "Bamberger's Helpers."

Liza submitted a budget for a demo schedule by department store chain, prioritizing locations that would give the highest return on investment: Bloomingdale's at The Falls in Miami, Gayfers at Regency Square in Jacksonville, Ivey's at Clearwater Mall, Jacobson's on Park Avenue in Winter Park, and Burdines Dadeland.

I made it a point to meet Liza's regulars, who would be the trainers sent to other cities nationwide as Liza licensed out her business model. There was Will in Orlando who came up with the idea to bring a paper doily to put under the plate holding the samples. Koko in Tampa came up with the idea to print a sign that said, "special sampling day," so customers did not think they could walk into a department store anytime they wanted and ask for a sample. Demonstrators carried the samples in with them; stores did not have any free sample inventory.

When I lived in Miami, I would look at the schedule and decide which stores to go to on weekends when demonstrators were working, to "mystery shop" Liza's recruits. To my pleasant surprise, things had never looked better. At Belk Lindsey, the demonstrator straightened up the Godiva display on arrival and found the signage that the department manager thought was "lost." At Dillard's the demonstrator retied any ribbons and bows that customers had untied to try to see what was in the box (which is impossible because there is a pad under the shrink wrap).

Without fail, there was a crowd around each Godiva display. It turns out people like free samples, especially Godiva! Commission salespeople would swoop in like vultures to help customers choose "the perfect gift." All in all, it was money well spent to activate the candy department considering the fact that chocolate has limited shelf life and needs to sell; otherwise, it is a markdown to the retailer.

Liza found her demonstrators in the most unlikely ways. One day at the Fort Lauderdale Galleria, Liza was putting out a Godiva order at Neiman Marcus. Elton John came in and wanted to buy about $20,000 worth of Godiva. But he didn't carry money. A woman with him named Charity had driven Elton John to the mall. (Liza was near enough to the cash register by the Godiva display that she heard the entire story and relayed it to me.) Charity pulled out her own Neiman Marcus charge card to pay for Elton John's items. The machine beeped. The sales associate called the credit department. The credit department asked the salesperson to put the customer on the line. Charity could be heard saying, "I know I don't usually spend that much... I'm helping Elton John do his shopping today... my husband is Elton John's tour manager... he works for Elton, Elton will give us the money before the bill even reaches us." That was all the credit department needed to hear!

With that, the salesclerk started bagging up the order. Liza helped Charity carry the order out to the car and made it a point to thank Charity for suggesting Godiva. Liza mentioned that she could use Charity as a demonstrator. Charity ended up staying on for more than ten years, eventually transferring to Los Angeles when I made the move west.

Charity became a supervisor for Liza's network of demonstrators in California and Florida and quickly found out she could choose from a pool of models and actors who needed side work to make extra money. Through Liza and Charity, I met Matt, Lyndon, Tyler, Rory, Candy, and Pruitt, all of whom were promoted to account coordinators, meaning they were hired by Godiva to work permanently on our payroll. Liza's team became the backbone of Godiva's sales support organization, handling whatever projects I threw their way in Godiva's two fastest-growing markets.

Realizing how resourceful Liza's crew could be, I wanted to test how far we could expand the scope of utilizing Liza's agency since her team were local "feet on the ground" that I sensed could be valuable to Godiva in other ways. I asked Liza to train Matt to be a "territory manager." I completely made that title up one day after meeting Matt and conversing with him. Matt could be the ambitious trainee who I'd have call on minor retail chains that exhibited the potential to expand exponentially if they were serviced properly. Full-fledged Godiva account executives earning million-dollar salaries could not be bothered with Harris, a small chain of department stores based around Palm Springs, for example. Account executives used to tell me that they "knew who buttered their bread," meaning they focused on the 80/20 rule of thumb—80 percent of sales came from 20 percent of customers. Yet the Harris buyer described their stores as upscale and regaled me with their plans to position Harris as the strongest independent chain of department stores in the Southwest. I figured for Matt, being able to make a few hundred thousand dollars in commissions might make it worth his while to trek out to Palm Springs and take the buyer to lunch a few times, write some orders, and work on production forecasts. Besides, employees had expense accounts, and Matt would be reimbursed for out-of-pocket expenses, so there would be "no harm, no foul" to this experiment.

Matt made his first call at Harris just before Father's Day one year. When he got home, Matt called me. "If we're going to open Harris, we may as well activate the 99 Cents Store," Matt said. He went on to describe how downscale the place was—which often happened when they called us, we didn't call them—and not up to Godiva standards in any way.

I was so happy to hear that Matt had made the decision that Godiva would *not* be opening a new account! The reality was my brand had such personality that Matt—or anyone on my team by that point—could innately assess which retail chains Godiva did or did not belong in. Matt knew Godiva had a distinct vibe, and Godiva's demographics were not a match with Harris's clientele.

The irony of Matt's decision is that nowadays, Godiva *is* sold at the 99 Cents Stores, and at the car wash, gas station, convenience store, and in many other retailers that Matt, Liza, Charity, and I would never have considered opening back in the day.

Some of Liza's sub-contractor agencies are still around today. The focus of those agencies must have pivoted since, to my knowledge, Godiva stopped offering samples decades ago. Nowadays, if you want to try Godiva, you have to buy a box.

I still wanted to try delegating more responsibilities to people working in field sales, so Liza introduced me to one of Matt's colleagues named Dan, who worked as the account coordinator overseeing stores selling Godiva in Tampa and Orlando. When one of Dan's stores sold out of Godiva one day, Dan created a display using mostly Godiva props from trade shows out of clear desperation. Dan accidentally created an entirely new way of marketing, called the "mini shop," which became Godiva's brand standard in retail chains.

It all started when the sister who co-owned Godiva was having a party at her home in horse country near Ocala. At the last minute she decided to give Godiva to her guests as a party favor. The store carrying Godiva nearest to her was Maas Brothers in Lakeland. She placed a phone order and took the entire inventory of whatever was in stock at the moment. A location had never completely sold out of Godiva before.

The shareholder's driver showed up and once his vehicle was loaded, Godiva's marquee refrigerated display case was sitting empty in a highly visible location of the nicest department store in Polk County. I received a call from Dan asking for suggestions about what to do.

"Unplug the case and move it to the stockroom," I said, "and put a potted plant or something there, to fill up the space. Then call the factory and place a re-order." An account coordinator had never placed an order before, which was one reason why I liked the direction this experiment was going: we received an instant re-order, and I was also excited about Dan's sales!

Dan found the dockmaster, who needed to bring the forklift into the store to lift the entire chocolate case onto a pallet. They wheeled it in back and stored it out of the way somewhere. Dan was told it would take two weeks for $20,000 worth of replenishment because rather than sending year-round gold ballotins, Lakeland would be the first US store to receive Godiva's new "Summer in Provence" collection. But Maas Brothers wouldn't let valuable floor space sit empty for two weeks.

Dan turned trash to treasure. He re-purposed some left-over trade show posters found in the trunk of his car parked outside. They read, "Godiva Coming Soon," "Founded in Belgium 1926," and "By Appointment to Her Majesty the Queen." Dan put two posters in the poster frames on the wall on either side of where the Godiva case should have been, and he placed another poster in a free-standing sign holder found in the visual manager's stockpile. Dan was staking his turf. Customers would know to shop this area of Maas Brothers when looking for chocolate.

Since there wasn't any chocolate for sale in the chocolate department, Dan had to deal with the dilemma I had created by going nationwide with dedicated Godiva fixturing. Our dedicated floor space had to be filled up to protect valuable square footage from being forfeited by default while also giving customers the impression that something new and exciting was on the way! Dan set up a banner, a six-foot-tall embroidered fabric scroll fitted into its own floor stand. Banners were used at the duty-free trade shows where booth space is tight, allowing for vertical signage when there is no wall.

The effect looked really good to me when I saw photos. Store management loved it. An idea was born! I decided all department stores should have a tool kit of this collateral to be able to be used as needed at the local level. From then on, Godiva's standard operating procedure became a policy of creating Godiva branded tablecloths, overlays, banners, posters, and POP (point of purchase) signs provided to the stores for free.

This was quite a cost to incur because, for example, if Macy's had 1,000 stores, and Macy's display in one store typically had two tables and two towers adjoining the Godiva case, Macy's would require 2,000 tablecloths, 2,000 overlays, 1,000 banners, 4,000 posters, and 4,000 POP tents.

I could not have foreseen the upside based on spontaneous reaction from department stores across the country. Visual managers loved having vendor-supplied, high-quality, branded materials to work with. Department stores started setting up "outposts." Rather than confining Godiva's display to the four-by-four-foot area surrounding our chocolate case, visual managers set up inexpensive "rounders" (which are lightweight tables that are extremely portable) all around the building wherever extra space could be found.

A cluster of two rounders in the jewelry department, covered by Godiva tablecloths and accompanied by a Godiva poster in a sign holder, created an "outpost" visually signaling that chocolate was a great gift idea. Godiva was being displayed all over the stores! I was getting pictures from account coordinators of Godiva displays in fragrances at the mall entrance, in men's suits, in the children's department, in housewares, in linens, and basically in any unused corner of the stores that needed a pop of color. But not only were these outposts helping retailers decorate their stores, merchandise was selling!

Customers were picking up a box of Godiva and walking to the cash register in gift wrap, the restaurant, the travel agency, the beauty salon, and all sorts of places Godiva never used to be. This led to us receiving more orders for product to fill up all the extra floor space.

A domino effect started by a store selling out its inventory, led to a chain of events that, in less than a year, reorganized the way Godiva was presented and sold at retail. Grabbing consumers' attention via this "headquarters effect" has been the way Godiva does business ever since. Thirty years later, I still see department stores featuring Godiva mini-shops anchoring multiple outposts throughout the building.

According to the Q scores we were paying for, mini-shops dramatically increased Godiva's noise level. (Q scores are used in Hollywood to rate a personality's or a brand's level of awareness and amount of media mentions, creating a popularity score in pop culture.) Godiva Chocolate and Waterford Crystal had always alternated between the number one and number two spots in Q score rankings for luxury goods ever since Q scores had begun being given for consumer products. Some years Godiva would be number one, some years Waterford would rank number one, but I do not recall any other brand ever bumping either Godiva or Waterford out of the top rankings for luxury goods. I took the position that high Q scores were another way of quantifying Godiva's marketing.

Chapter 6

I SAW LADY GODIVA IN MIDTOWN

Now that Godiva was firmly entrenched in its own real estate following roll-out of the mini-shop concept in department stores, we had a lot of real estate to fill. But there was more to it than that. My desire was to create a year-round business to smooth out cash flow, manufacturing, and workload. As recently as the early 1980s, under my predecessor, Godiva did business with retail chains who only displayed Godiva products at holidays, shipping product when the retailer decided to carry chocolate such as at Christmas, Valentine's Day, and Easter. I found that to be ludicrous. As I kept saying, we were building a brand. A brand does not just vanish from stores for much of the year; customers need to have access to a brand's products at their convenience.

Contracts were updated to require stores to order and display Godiva year-round, no more "cherry-picking" the line. Each account was required to maintain a representative sample of Godiva's entire product portfolio of boxed chocolate, chocolate bars, and other new items I will be describing throughout this chapter. Only a few retailers would not commit to maintaining a permanent Godiva presence, and those dropped Godiva. A notable example was The Broadway in Los Angeles. Other retailers in those markets quickly picked up the clientele, so this decision was a complete non-conversation. Retailers I talked to said it made sense.

I was familiar with the type of brand extensions that began before I arrived at Godiva. Both Godiva Liquor and Godiva Cheesecake pre-dated me. The liquor was marketed by Seagram's and had been sold in liquor stores and bars for years. Cheesecake Factory sold the cheesecake in its restaurants. Those were pure licensing deals—"mailbox money." Godiva sold the rights to use its name on products manufactured by other companies. Godiva had no involvement and no responsibilities. Godiva received a check every quarter based on a percentage of sales for use of the Godiva name.

My plan was to invent varied Godiva products that could be sold alongside chocolate. Doing so would bring in new revenue streams, diversify Godiva's portfolio, and engage the customer with new and interesting gift ideas in our rapidly expanding mecca of display cases, tables, and towers. This was not a matter of developing new flavors of chocolates. I was searching for related consumables, which we could market as luxury goods with relatively long shelf lives that could fit into Godiva's existing distribution network. I brainstormed starting with Godiva Water, for example, because Americans were starting to carry water bottles with them everywhere.

Rather than Godiva's research and development team or the marketing folks heading up the brand extension endeavor, I started backwards and did something Godiva had never done. I asked the salespeople to be my "task force" and come up with suggestions for products they felt might be well-received if packaged properly and priced right. The brief made clear that I was going in a different direction. To capture full retail margins as opposed to slim licensing percentages, we'd "co-pack," defined as having experts in a product category produce and package for us under the Godiva name and ship to Godiva's warehouse. Godiva's distribution logistics had to be able to deliver the new products along with standard chocolate shipments, all ordered on a single combined PO. I wanted to present the illusion that Godiva was making in-house whatever new products we decided to launch.

But I was not averse to licensing deals either, provided licensed products sold outside normal Godiva channels. Liquor and cheesecakes were not sold in department stores, and chocolates were not sold in liquor stores, restaurants, or bars. I needed to define a firewall to help the sales force understand under what circumstances they would have to do the selling. If a new product category was developed for our traditional channels, Godiva would have a third party produce and package the new product for us, ship to us, and we would pay them. Such co-packers acted solely in the role of manufacturers because under that scenario, Godiva's sales force would write orders. The other option, licensing products, meant Godiva never owned the product and would not be selling it.

Department stores were quite predictable in regards to their product assortment plans in the gourmet food department. Many chains offered Godiva Chocolates, Downey's Cakes, and Bahlsen Cookies. Customers had a choice of chocolates, cakes, or cookies. This observation provided a clue. Godiva's first brand extension was cakes. Godiva Liquor Cakes were sold in gold tins. They were Bundt cakes seeped in liquors designed for entertaining. The flavors were yellow cake with amaretto, chocolate cake with brandy, and white cake with Chambord. Pricing was about twenty dollars for a one-pound cake, which was very expensive at that time. Reaction from retailers was ho-hum, and customers kind of shrugged. What we learned was Godiva was not known for cakes, and two-thirds of our cake product offering did not contain chocolate. This experiment was too much of a disconnect. Cakes were discontinued after one holiday season.

The next year a major distributor of ice cream to supermarkets nationwide approached Godiva about creating Godiva Ice Cream under a pure licensing arrangement. We said yes, because this time around, ice cream would not be sold in Godiva's boutiques. There were pints and quarts in various chocolate flavors. However, Godiva Ice Cream turned up in convenience stores across the US, and in gas stations, truck stops, and in all types of supermarkets, not just the high-end specialty grocers I had envisioned would be the target market. It turned out the key word I had overlooked was "distributor." The distributor was having the ice cream made and selling it along with numerous other ice cream brands they represented. The distributor did not care where the ice cream was sold; their game was numbers. Mass distribution was contrary to my brand management. That contract was not renewed because I did not want the Godiva name to lose its exclusivity.

Godiva Ice Cream has been resurrected at least two more times since my days at Godiva. The idea comes and goes. Thirty years later it seems like there is still a desire to make it work.

Godiva launched coffee next. It was branded Café Godiva. Coffee satisfied all of our requirements. We had arabica beans roasted, ground, and flavored, sealed in stand-up vacuum pouches in two sizes (single pot and twelve ounce). Coffee was easy to ship as a non-perishable and displayed beautifully on Godiva gondolas adjacent to Godiva's chocolate cases. Shelf-life was one year. Godiva offered regular and decaffeinated plus flavors including chocolate, hazelnut, and cinnamon. Pricing was about three dollars for a single-pot trial size and fifteen dollars for the twelve-ounce bag. For contrast, we chose a blue bag with black Godiva lettering. That was a huge mistake. The blue looked dark in stores, and the logo was hard to see, plus customers expected Godiva to be gold. As soon as the initial order of packaging was depleted, we switched to brilliant bright gold bags with black lettering. Café Godiva in a sparkly light brown design is still available now, but at some point, department stores seem to have gotten out of the Café Godiva business.

Café Godiva is the best coffee there is, and I highly recommend it. Repeat purchases were staggering. Coffee was a day-in/day-out, year-round business. The individual size became an impulse purchase. Sales of the large size surged as a gift solution around the holidays. We could not have been happier with the results. Godiva powered forward with more brand extensions as coffee proved to us that consumers would accept Godiva's name on products other than chocolate.

Godiva Hot Chocolate was introduced the next year. Hot chocolate packets were sold in both a box and a tin containing several packets. Consumers added milk and heated it on the stove or in the microwave. Godiva Hot Chocolate was a no-brainer, but I am glad we did not lead with hot chocolate because to me, it was not an industry-leading preparation. The quality of the ingredients in the packet was extraordinary, but the powder was still a mix and not actual chocolate. I wanted to explore chunks of solid chocolate flakes to melt or a liquid chocolate syrup base sold in a jar. Years before, when I worked in the buying office, Godiva marketed jars of chocolate syrup as ice cream topping. My preference was to bring back that old program under a new name. The issue was pricing: using any of my ideas would have pushed retail hot cocoa prices above coffee prices, and that simply would not work. The sales force was telling me hot chocolate would be a children's item and had to be priced on the low end. They were correct, and Godiva Hot Chocolate is still sold today.

I decided to focus on brand extensions that could seriously move the needle in terms of sales and profits. It took just as much time and effort to create a low-selling category (hot cocoa) as it did to generate a high-selling category (coffee). Incremental sales were all adding up, making the effort worth our while. Coffee sales hit 10 percent of chocolate sales by year two. Re-evaluating the department store triumvirate of chocolate, cakes, and cookies, it seemed like cookies should be next.

Cookies would be sold globally (whereas Café Godiva was a US-only product line). There was a very good reason why that decision evolved. Godiva was owned by Campbell's Soup—who also owned Pepperidge Farm Cookies, one of the most beloved brands of all time (as was Campbell's Soup). Pepperidge Farm was a much bigger business for Campbell's than Godiva, and I could not get anyone's attention. They had no interest—none—in baking a selection of cookies for their "sister" company Godiva. I was flat out dismissed by the head of Pepperidge Farm, who told me, "Godiva couldn't do the volume."

That was the wrong thing to say to the person charged with growing Godiva into a global brand.

I approached Pepperidge Farms' competitor, headquartered in New Jersey, the US division of Europe's biggest cookie company. Management there was deliriously eager to make a deal. Their team developed a line of chocolate-covered cookies. One cookie had Godiva's logo stamped in the chocolate on top! Everything was delicious, the packaging was spectacular, shelf-life was fine because of vacuum-packing, and pricing met our targets. But the cookie co-packer would only begin production if they could produce enough to deliver to Godiva's warehouses in Brussels and Philadelphia since they sought immense distribution to blast past Pepperidge Farm in sales.

I agreed to sell Godiva's cookies worldwide, which necessitated a name change from our working title. We called the product, Godiva Biscuits, because in Europe the word "biscuits" means cookies, and in the US, "biscuits" sounded upscale in focus groups.

The head of Pepperidge Farm must have discovered my plan because he called complaining, "You went with a competitor!" sounding like a coach who thought he called the plays.

"I sure did. And what are *you* going to do about it?" I retorted, meaning he forgot I was paid top dollar to nurture the Godiva brand, which meant I had a green light from *my* shareholders who owned *his* brand too! (Godiva was not going to be held hostage by Pepperidge Farm.)

This was a common theme throughout my career. People needed to get the memo that I was the one who wrote the endings to my stories.

Specifically regarding Godiva Biscuits, the ending to that story has been written for over two decades. Godiva Biscuits are sold everywhere today globally. I buy them all the time. Absolutely nothing about them has changed! The shapes, the flavors, the box—everything—is identical to what I signed off on.

The contract with the biscuit manufacturer specifically carved out biscotti because I wanted to do something different with biscotti as a tie-in with Café Godiva. Godiva retained the rights to sell Godiva Biscotti as a completely separate product line, which we did the following year. Stores merchandised biscotti on the towers alongside coffee and hot cocoa in the stores. Biscuits were always displayed on their own on a stand-alone fixture. Biscotti has also survived all these years and are especially popular in gift baskets.

By that point there was no more room in a typical department store or Godiva boutique to add any additional fixturing to accommodate further brand extensions. Godiva had achieved my goal of establishing a presence as a complete "family" of related products in stores. Sales were up another 10 percent after the addition of biscuits. I stopped pushing because the danger could become distraction if we diverted our attention from the core chocolate business. People never stopped suggesting brand extensions though. It has been interesting in recent years to watch Godiva's resurgence into licensing. Recently, supermarkets have launched Godiva cake mixes, Godiva pudding, and Godiva baked goods.

The very fact that so many brand extensions were possible speaks to the power of Godiva's brand. I kept stressing the importance of building a brand rather than selling products because such an ideology formed the framework for continuous expansion without the need for extensive capital. We kept simplicity in mind. Godiva's self-service business in department stores taught us our packaging had to convey everything the customer needed to know in order to decide to buy our products. Most importantly, all of the new brand extensions were year-round items.

That meant the time was right to go back to Godiva's roots. Years' worth of various food and drink brand extensions meant it was time to start thinking about refreshing Godiva Chocolates.

The master chocolatier had been wanting to start selling new "nut butters." These were Godiva's foil-wrapped rectangular pieces of cashew butter, hazelnut butter, and almond butter. The nuts were caramelized—meaning roasted with brown sugar—and then pureed until smooth with milk chocolate added. This was a very common chocolate style in Europe.

Godiva's advertising agency pitched me an idea for nut butter TV commercials. Lady Godiva would be a citizen of the 1990s, acting as a spokesmodel for "her" chocolate. The character would be portrayed by an actress wearing a long flowing wig. The motivation" in the commercial would be for Lady Godiva to hold up boxes of Godiva Chocolate and talk about how proud she was of her legacy. It was kind of going to be like Godiva's version of Mrs. Field's advertising her cookies. The ad campaign sounded contemporary and fun, and it seemed unique because only Godiva could pull it off.

I arranged to be in New York for the filming of the commercial. The studios were in buildings off Madison Avenue that were formerly the original CBS Television Network studios in Midtown. Ironically, there was a Leonidas Chocolate store on the ground floor of the building. A block up and over was Rockefeller Center, where Godiva and Teuscher had flagship stores.

The three-camera shoot spared no expense because Godiva was paying for it, of course. The agency had seated a live studio audience to energize the actress as she filmed her scenes. There were no less than twenty staffers on set, meticulously planning every detail, saying things like, "She wants the box angled up ten degrees into the camera," and "Her cue cards need to be written in Times New Roman font." Good, I thought to myself, they hired an actress who is somewhat of a perfectionist and knows how to organize things to get the scene done quickly with no overtime. At that point I had not yet met whoever was to portray "Lady Godiva." I wanted to see the character come to life from the vantage point of the audience for the first time when the actress entered her scene from backstage. I sat on a folding chair behind the cameraman, under microphones lowered from the ceiling and Broadway-style stage lights.

The narrator spoke to the audience from a microphone. "Ladies and gentlemen, you are about to see what we are sure will be an award-winning performance, as Godiva Chocolate brings you their newest spokesmodel, Lady Godiva!"

The audience started applauding, the crew took their positions, and the director yelled, "Action!"

"Lady Godiva Chocolates, scene one, take one," the person said, holding the thing that snaps closed at the beginning of a movie shoot. (I hated it when the name of the company was stated incorrectly.)

As soon as everybody moved out of the way, I could see the actress for the first time. It was Mrs. Phoebe van Rensylier! The shareholder of Godiva was playing Lady Godiva!

They had done a good job. In addition to theatrical makeup and an outlandish wig, she was wearing a St. John two-piece suit knitted in shimmery gold, which gave the appearance of someone in great shape. Mrs. van Rensylier's Lily Pulitzer shoes with matching gold straps were immediately recognizable. When I looked into the monitor and saw how the director was shooting Lady Godiva with a filtered lens, it was magical. On film she appeared to be in her thirties or forties. In actuality she might have been ten years older.

The commercial was over in thirty seconds. The producer did two more takes, why—I don't know.

After it was over, I said to the agency rep, "Take me back to Lady Godiva's dressing room."

We went backstage, and I knocked. "Mrs. R," as I always called her, "it's Brad."

"Entrée!" she said, and we went in.

As the agency rep started to introduce us, I interrupted, "We already know each other."

"We sure do; you can say that again." Mrs. R said emphatically. "Now both of you sit down."

(She always got straight to the point.)

We sat in two chairs while, still in full costume, Mrs. R balanced on the arm of the settee as best she could in the get-up and the wig, mimicking what she might look like if galloping off holding onto her horse. The scene was surreal; we were "talking" to Lady Godiva.

She insisted, "Listen up. You better believe if I'm going to invest two hundred million dollars to grow this brand of chocolate, my picture better be on every box. You're going to put me through hair, makeup, and wardrobe for every commercial from now on, and then shoot me with a soft lens, and photoshop the pictures after that. Because I want to look good, and no matter what, I intend to be immortalized in history as *Lady Godiva*. From now on *I* am the face of this brand."

I thought, "So, that is what this is about. Mrs. R wants to see her name in lights." I would never have imagined that a prominent socialite from the proper socio-economic background had aspirations to be an actress, or a model, or a "star."

I went back to Los Angeles thinking this idea was so much fun! The studio audience loved it.

The Godiva team began creating hang-tags with a photo of Mrs. R as Lady Godiva in a filigree swirl. The hang-tag would be ribboned around each box of Godiva.

But Godiva was having problems with nut butters. The chocolates were not molded, they were sliced into rectangular blocks in the style of German marzipan or Italian torrone. This made them heavy. As a result, we calculated we were not making any profit. Nut butters were not selling in stores anyway because they did not look pretty in the traditional Belgian style.

In the factory, the little blocks of nut butter maintained their shape within the precisely cool temperatures of the plant. But in stores, nut butters could not stack. Pieces started to flatten, sink, and spread. That caused the foil wrappers to open, letting messy nut butter leak out.

I ordered a stop-down on production, the first time I had done that. No more nut butters would be manufactured.

The ad campaign never ran. This was a case of "putting the cart before the horse," (pun intended). Nut butters were discontinued, so Godiva had no use for a nut butter ad campaign.

Mrs. R seemed to have lost interest because I never heard another suggestion from either her or our agency to try again with the Lady Godiva character. The character rode off into the sunset.

But I still believed more innovation in chocolates was possible because Godiva's organization was under-utilized. We were a $350-million-a-year business with the bandwidth to easily support a $1-billion-a-year business with no further investment in people or equipment. My opinion was that expanding the chocolate line would definitely not create a situation where Godiva was inventing its own competition. Wholesale customers yearned for additional luxury chocolates positioned above Godiva. There were infinite competitors positioned below Godiva. None of them were in a position to leap-frog over us. We had to be the ones to lead the market further upscale.

The most monumental new product launch Godiva made since its inception was the next pair of chocolate brand extensions "extraordinaire" that most people will not remember. Going into the new millennium, Godiva decided to act on my idea to create two entirely new lines of chocolate. These were called G and Platinum, two distinct ultra-luxury chocolate brands.

In a sentence: my plan was to move up the price point for "regular" Godiva. "G" was launched twenty-five dollars per pound above Godiva. "Platinum" was launched another twenty-five dollars per pound above "G." Godiva had taken a price increase to fifty dollars per pound. For once and for all, customers stopped complaining that Godiva was too expensive. Fifty dollars per pound provided real value compared to seventy-five dollars per pound and one hundred dollars per pound labels.

Exclusive retailers Holt-Renfrew in Canada, Bergdorf Goodman in New York, Harrods in London, and Galleries Lafayette in Paris, were stopped in their tracks from complaining that Godiva had become too accessible. Yes, Godiva had chased volume over the years and opened many new sales points, but now a tool existed for Godiva to reward upper-echelon retailers. G and Platinum were linked to Godiva, meaning that G and Platinum were only offered to top-tier retail partners who met stratospheric Godiva sales targets. What that accomplished was ensuring only the aforementioned Godiva customers could qualify for the rights to carry G and Platinum. They were happy. G and Platinum became an exclusive club that was not open to ordinary Godiva wholesale accounts.

The genesis for my idea originated when I wondered out loud why Godiva's sales force couldn't go into buying office meetings with a secondary brand to sell. Godiva reps had *access*. The door was always open for them. My sales force was golden. But they had time on their hands between meetings, and we could reduce about 75 percent of their paperwork. The factories outside Philadelphia and in Brussels were by this time benefitting from the use of back-up warehouses in Canada under NAFTA, freeing up former storage space. There was room to do so much more in terms of manufacturing. The master chocolatier was always full of ideas.

Ultimately, start-up costs for two new brands would be no more than a relatively modest line-item in the annual budget, which was offset by a reduction in marketing spend during year one. Most of the budget went to creating all new G and Platinum packaging. Chocolate manufacturing cost the same whether the factory was making Godiva, G, or Platinum. Under LCBS (least cost business systems), if the cost of sugar went up, a less expensive milk supplier would be found because at the end of the day, production costs were going to remain stable. Nobody else could have done what Godiva did.

The plan was for only the top 10 percent of Godiva's own boutiques to sell G and Platinum. The new brands were to be *that* exclusive. I think that is where the challenges began. G and Platinum could not gain traction because Godiva's die-hard customer base never knew either existed. The department stores selling G and Platinum also had limited footprints. Unexpectedly, some accounts we had in mind to stock both G and Platinum chose to only carry one or the other.

Reviews came in basically questioning whether G and Platinum were targeting too thin a slice of the public. Could the average person who wanted a box of chocolate discern any difference between Godiva, G, Platinum, or any other Belgian brand, or possibly any European brand? Adding to the fact that extremely limited distribution made G and Platinum hard to buy, when a customer did discover either collection, sales associates in stores could not articulate a distinction between G and Platinum. People were asking: "Why were both needed?"

The first reason was in keeping with flavor profiles. The types of chocolates in the G and Platinum collections were hand-made chocolates, not machine-made confections. Unique garnishes provided eye appeal. Platinum consisted of exotic fillings, varying cocoa intensities, and single-origin chocolate. G was an elevated traditional chocolate experience.

The second reason had to do with creating understated, simple packaging. The idea was for household staff to buy these chocolates using house money. The target market was not the end consumer. G and Platinum were expected to be presented out of the box displayed on a silver tray or candy dish for passing to guests.

With very little marketing emphasis placed on G and Platinum, the market revealed customers preferred to buy two boxes of Godiva rather than one box of Platinum. The public was beginning to shop by piece count. We noticed the same phenomenon at Godiva boutiques in Europe. Godiva introduced a one kilo ballotin there in response to the increase in transactions whereby shoppers bought two 500-gram ballotins to get the number of pieces of chocolate they needed. The legacy of G and Platinum is Godiva now pricing chocolate by the piece instead of by the pound in retail stores. Instead of a "one-pound box," the labeling identifies the package as a "thirty-piece box." Individual pieces are sold as "each" rather than being weighed on a scale.

G and Platinum lasted several years. Since being discontinued, the "G" and "Platinum" names have been recycled by Godiva many times in the years since, but in later usage neither term refers to the two standalone collections referenced here.

Chapter 7

WHAT THE TYPE OF CHOCOLATE YOU EAT SAYS ABOUT YOUR PERSONALITY

During my era at Godiva, when people moved, they had to get a new phone number. Computers were in use at businesses, but not by households. Godiva began to use the internet in 1997 but only to transmit sales figures and order details back and forth between the factory and the stores, not for any social reasons. Looking around, I began to suspect that the term "technology" was going to mean different things to different industries.

When talking with colleagues at the time about their attitudes towards new technologies, I sensed a wariness based on vague feelings that IT was thought of as a bogeyman coming to make work harder by causing frustration and exasperation. I knew that meant I needed to gradually phase in new technological advances one step at a time. All projects were tackled in-house so that customized training was conducted by and among Godiva departments.

The undercurrent was my insistence that employees under my watch would always be given the opportunity to gain new skills. I remember calling associates and saying my famous line, "You are not going to be left behind." That meant learning how to use the computer was important in a way that made us seem like family. As soon as people made time to switch over to the new way of doing things, they realized that, rather than becoming harder, work was being simplified. The main reasons this approach worked were because: a.) systems I implemented really did make jobs easier; b.) we made sure training was fun by streamlining and simplifying; and c.) everyone knew there were no alternatives; tech was here to stay.

I began by prioritizing which technologies could be applied to marketing luxury chocolates. Nowadays, I would have a CTO (Chief Technology Officer) do it, but back in the day, it was up to me. Virtually all of my ideas, which seemed high-tech at the time, are now baseline and commonplace in business. This placed Godiva in a leadership position in the industry as our standards became industry standards once competitors realized that retailers had become accustomed to expecting the new technology.

"A business with no signs is a sign of no business," was one of my mottos. It explained my reasoning for supplying stores with branded price signs that could be put up in so many ways there could be no doubt how much a box of Godiva cost. Believe it or not, we had abdicated the responsibility for applying price tags to the retailers. In those days retailers used a hand-held ticketing gun to apply a small sticker to the bottom of each box. I considered a price tag to be a small sign of sorts. So, first up in the technological revolution was price tags.

UPC bar codes had just been introduced. The UCC—Uniform Code Council—in Washington, DC, issued UPC's for $1,000 per batch by correlating the first few digits of the bar code to a specific manufacturer. Godiva printed UPC bar codes showing the retail price as well. That way we could pre-ticket each box of chocolate as it came down the assembly line, saving stores a step when unpacking their orders.

My goal was for the UPC price tag to be removable because Godiva is given as a gift. I believed my UPC solution was very classy. We developed a two-layer UPC sticker. The easy pull-off top layer had the price printed on it. The sticky bottom layer was the same gold color as Godiva's boxes. The net result was that customers could easily pull off the price tag without ripping the surface of the box.

Behind the scenes the retailer was able to track a lot of information about our inventory once the UPC was scanned. Department store buyers knew which sizes of boxes were best-sellers at the push of a key on their computers at the office. Reports totaled daily Godiva sales by branch. I started asking a lot of questions from a marketing perspective to see what else could be learned about Godiva from UPC data.

Some retail partners were more willing than others to share details about traffic patterns in their stores. But certain trends were unmistakable. A high percentage of sales consisted of cosmetics and chocolate, lingerie and chocolate, and fashion jewelry and chocolate. Women were buying Godiva! (We had always thought men were purchasing chocolate for women.)

Zip code information gleaned from customers charging purchases on the retailers' own in-house credit cards was registered automatically by the computers at major holding companies such as ADG (Associated Dry Goods), Mercantile Stores, and Allied Stores. Major retailers were just beginning to experiment with what knowledge they could extract about their customers' habits through this new technology. This information enabled Godiva to determine average household income by zip code, distance driven to malls, and average amount spent per trip. The huge takeaway for Godiva was that chocolate was clearly an add-on purchase. Few-to-no customers drove to the mall just to buy a box of chocolates.

With that information at hand, Godiva began encouraging chain stores to display chocolates on top of the purse display, the watch display, the perfume display, and any other counter that was near a register. I decided Godiva needed to behave more like other luxury European brands which marketed themselves at point-of-sale with extensive collateral. We printed white Godiva bags with gold ribbon handles and shipped the bags free to department stores. The retailers would distribute the bags throughout the building to various registers. That way, each sales associate could make a grand presentation to their customer by placing Godiva purchases in a Godiva bag.

Switching over to UPC's was the easiest first step to take on the technology journey because everyone agreed the time had come to implement it. It took me about a year to figure out what we could do next. Staff had their opinions, and I had to sort through a variety of proposals and do a cost-benefit analysis of the finalists.

The next ground-breaking technology I implemented was EDI (Electronic Data Interchange). EDI is a system linking each department store's computer directly to Godiva's computer. At midnight each night, a retailer's computer could transmit an order to Godiva untouched by human hands. EDI meant we did not have to chase down the candy buyer to write a PO for replenishment on never-out basics. Godiva programmed the case packs into EDI (for example, twelve one-pound boxes per case). Godiva also programmed the minimum order quantity into EDI (for example, one case). So, if Maison Blanche in New Orleans sold twelve one-pound boxes of Godiva, Maison Blanche's computer automatically placed a re-order for a case of one-pound boxes with the New Orleans store's shipping address using EDI.

Investing in EDI technology had to be a two-way street. Godiva could not transmit orders via EDI if there was nowhere for the orders to be sent! I forged a path by networking with leadership from several apparel, china, and linen manufacturers. Together this achieved the critical mass of vendors necessary to convince department stores to actually implement EDI. Godiva was able to become a much nimbler organization from an inventory perspective once EDI began to be used by several chains. We evolved to being more of a "just-in-time" producer.

Within no more than two years, all major US department stores had installed EDI—not just for Godiva of course. This greatly streamlined the re-ordering process with the added unexpected benefit of freeing up a lot of the account executives' time to pursue business development with potential new accounts.

Prior to EDI, we produced only enough seasonal items to fulfill initial orders; no re-orders were possible. For the first time, EDI allowed Godiva to fulfill never-out-basic reorders generated by EDI as replenishment for sold-out seasonal goods. Prior to EDI, if Halloween sold out early in the season, for example, good luck trying to get an appointment with the buyer in time to write a basic replenishment order using available open-to-buy. There was never enough time to get the order approved, and ship the order with any reasonable expectation of the re-order selling-through before

Christmas goods arrived. EDI took care of all that by generating replenishment orders daily!

EDI caused us to consider which aspects of Godiva's product line could be considered "year-round." We doubled the number of SKUs (Stock Keeping Units) in the product line that the factory kept on-hand for immediate re-stocking. During this period, 1997–1999, implementation of EDI took sales from about $175 million to about $200 million in the US. And the sales reps *loved* it because they earned commissions on every shipment, even those generated on behalf of their customers by EDI!

I had to personalize "the computer," as people called it that first year. There was rampant fear that "the computer" was going to take peoples' jobs away or mess up an order and somehow ruin Godiva's reputation with a key retailer. My take on how to handle this was to simply "friendly-up" "the computer" by giving it human names. I chose Nancy North, Evelyn East, Sue South, and Wendy West. I hired four customer service reps and from the time they were hired, each of these ladies were to be known by their "computer" names. Their job was to monitor what the computer was doing in their assigned geographic territories of the US. This provided peace of mind to both Godiva's sales force and to the retail candy buyers, who at the outset were worried that the computer system might try to re-order the wrong chocolate.

It did take about one full year to smooth out the inventory highs and lows as we adapted to EDI. Since we had classified so many more SKUs as eligible to ship under EDI, we did not have sales history to lean on. Frankly, I told the factory to just put longer "best by" date codes on the outside of all the cartons. This took the angst out of maximizing production capacity. The factory made a lot more of whatever it was they were producing with no fear of it expiring before EDI sold it and shipped it.

Keeping a lot more inventory on-hand led directly to the next big technology improvement, which at that point absolutely had to happen, or Godiva would not have been in compliance with changing FDA requirements for "freshness codes."

Up to that point Godiva had always used "closed dating" because some people in Godiva's marketing department took the old-fashioned approach that the public would not understand the relationship between production dates, "best by" dates, and freshness for a consumable brand outside of a supermarket channel. Closed dating was a scrambled code printed on the bottom of each box of Godiva that could only be deciphered by Godiva field reps or factory staff.

I, on the other hand, sensed the world was evolving towards a "news you can use" era where consumers viewed marketing information as necessary in order to make an informed buying decision.

So, I invested in new optical character printers to use what was exciting technology at the time: dot matrix printing. Boxes of Godiva coming down the line at the factory were rapidly printed with an "open date code," a small purple line of text in English saying "use by" followed by a date which would be a few months out from the date of production. This meant people in stores could buy with confidence knowing their box of Godiva was the freshest possible chocolate. Customers could actually read the "use by" date. (In the food industry, this practice became known as "open dating.")

Little did I know these technological enhancements would soon have a global impact on Godiva's ability to market chocolate in new international sales territories. Japan was a leader in retail supply chain logistics. It would have been impossible to do business in Japan without UPC bar codes, EDI, and open dating. Now that Godiva had all three, we began test marketing in Tokyo.

Japanese customers are very different than US or European customers. The Japanese shopper picks up a box of chocolate, and if they do not see a best-by date, they will put the box down. Whereas in the US, a long best-by date far off in the future could be a customer's least important consideration; in Tokyo that would be the first consideration.

Japanese retailers use a notorious system of distributors for replenishment in order to keep store shelves stocked. There are layers of middlemen who all handle the goods. Doing so is systemic and ingrained philosophically as part of Japan's belief in full employment. Any way the Japanese can think of to create more jobs means more people work. UPCs and EDI are standard in Japan because both are integral to the movement of goods through various warehouses. (In fact, in Japan, all the people who handle products along the way to the store help market the brand. There is a word-of-mouth publicity system in back channels in Japan that does not have a parallel phenomenon in the US.) Through the use of the new technology, Godiva was able to fit into the established pipeline for the flow of goods in Japan.

Test sales in Japan were strong enough for me to establish an Asian sales office in Tokyo. (At the time of this writing, the Japanese division of Godiva that I started had been sold for $1 billion! While I cannot comment on how they arrived at that figure, the possibilities seem endless for the buyer to expand across Asia.)

When we first started shipping Godiva to Japan, the chocolates had to ship from Godiva's factory in Brussels. The master chocolatier in Brussels understood why we needed special flavors specifically for Japan. I had to be able to market a localized version of Godiva that people would actually buy. The first new flavor I approved was Green Tea, which proved very popular. We had Rooibos Mochi, which sold well there. But the mega-hit was chocolate with pineapple and macadamia nut, inspired by Hawaii, which is a popular destination for Japanese tourists.

My trips to Tokyo, Nagoya, and Osaka led to coming up with my theory that the type of chocolate a person eats says a lot about their personality. I saw Japanese culture as being team-oriented, polite, and rooted in customs. Younger people deferred to older people. Handing someone a business card involved a specific protocol of accepting it with two hands and actually looking at the card.

I recall a conversation with the chocolate buyer at Hanshin Department Store in Osaka. Through an interpreter (since I do not speak Japanese), I pointed out that dark chocolate with a cocoa percentage of 80 percent or more is metabolized by the body the same as a sugar-free product would. She agreed! The buyer said anybody in the chocolate industry would know that. But her questions were focused on the marketing aspect of how we would present that fact to the public.

The one subject I have been harassed about more than any other topic in the world of chocolate has been sugar-free chocolate. (Now the category is known as "no sugar added.") Originally, Godiva did not have a sugar-free line. I always held the opinion that taking the sugar out of the recipe would change the taste, the experience, and therefore, the brand. My belief had been that someone who could not eat sugar or did not want much sugar should simply enjoy a smaller piece of regular Godiva Chocolate. There was no need for a sugar-free Godiva Chocolate since the potential audience, I thought, was miniscule.

What came out of these trips was the origin of a new marketing philosophy that was based on targeted marketing or focused marketing. People have their reasons for wanting to choose vegan, Kosher, or sugar-free, and my job was going to be to juggle the budget to come up with enough money to splinter Godiva's marketing to reach each niche. Godiva marketing quickly evolved from using Godiva's standard campaigns globally, to tailored ads by country. The focus changed to specific product attributes, which benefitted the buyer. For example, Godiva's new sugar-free chocolate meant diabetics could now buy Godiva.

The single biggest change in marketing during my tenure was segmenting Godiva's marketing to attract casual buyers with snacking chocolate. This meant that, for the first time ever, I intended for Godiva to develop a "self-consumption business". (The term "self-consumption" referred to products we'd market to people who wanted to buy some chocolate to eat themselves, not to give as a gift.) I had the research and development team come up with sugar-free bars, high protein nut clusters, and Kosher bridge mix, to start.

We created single-serving sizes and all new packaging. The first item was a caramel nut cluster we named a Bouchee (the French word for "bite"). It was anything but a bite. Our Bouchee was about the size of what some manufacturers refer to as a "turtle," which took me about four bites to eat. We had done a lot of marketing research and discovered that the profile of Godiva self-consumption shoppers was going to be completely different than what we were accustomed to when marketing to traditional Godiva customers shopping for gifts.

The self-consumption customer was more active. They were interested in health and wellness but did not mind splurging calories on a product bearing the Godiva name. Self-consumption customers did not care about presentation at all; they'd tear the wrapper off and chomp into the chocolate immediately. I likened it to having the mind-set that chocolate was being consumed as a foodstuff for energy rather than as a treat.

Godiva was actually getting a glimpse into the psyche of what the type of chocolate a person eats says about their personality. White chocolate was generally deemed healthy during focus groups of this era. The connotation was that white chocolate had fewer calories or fat than milk chocolate, which had milk added, meaning white chocolate was "pure" chocolate. Scientifically, that is not factually correct. White chocolate starts as pure cocoa fat, meaning it is 100 percent fat. Then sugar and vanilla are added to give it flavor. But Godiva was going to market it based on the healthy perception.

We launched individually-sized snack packages of Godiva "panned" chocolates. (Panning is a less-expensive manufacturing process that allows for high-volume production and quicker turnaround time to get a product to market.) I did not want to risk a failure in the US if this self-consumption collection were to be a flop, so we launched it in Canada first. The marketing department was too aggressive about the campaign date, so we had limited quantities ready to ship in time. I was wondering if that was a good or bad thing.

Godiva white chocolate covered raisins and nuts could best be described as a "bridge mix." To me, the idea of a bridge mix was incongruous to the Godiva brand because Godiva was known for beautiful molded pieces of filled chocolate, not irregularly-shaped crunchy bits that were unidentifiable until you bit into them. Yet the test marketing was positive. I had not understood at first what the market was telling us: people wanted portable food with individual-sized packaging to keep in a pocket or purse or glove compartment for when hunger pangs arrived. These portion-controlled packages were also great for handing out to children.

Of all the lines I introduced, this one surprised me the most. The reason I say that is because the uses were so non-traditional for the brand. Godiva marketing needed to spearhead a metamorphosis from being a special occasion chocolate for entertaining and holiday gifting to being a daily indulgence.

I think what I learned from that experience is that marketing research is only as good as the effectiveness of the marketing team who is summarizing the report and communicating to management. I'm glad someone spoke up! To this day, I still see Godiva selling an updated version of the Bouchee collection. Godiva has adapted the little balls of chocolate as circular mints in white, milk, and dark chocolate. The packaging is now a tin, barely larger than the size of a package of gum.

In Canada the test results encouraged Godiva to broaden distribution channels. Bouchées in department stores barely sold, but Bouchées merchandised in a specialty food store sold out! Godiva "self-consumption" products needed to be available for purchase at places people frequented more often than malls. That was the year we approached Fresh Market, Wally's Wines, and Hudson Group among many other non-traditional outlets for us including Houdini, the biggest wholesale gift basket company in America, for example, about carrying Godiva.

It was during this era that I never stopped talking about chocolate. Whenever I met someone—at the gym, at a party, while travelling—I'd ask what kind of chocolate they liked and which mall they shopped at. (Subconsciously, I think I knew that someday I would write a book.) I have become very good at reading a person based on their answers to these two questions. I'm a dark chocolate lover who shops at free-standing department stores in Beverly Hills, for example. That is a specific demographic. Now form a picture in your mind of how I might shop versus a person who buys milk chocolate at a mall in Idaho.

The public does not care much for the term *demographics* because people do not like being considered as merely a small piece of a larger group. But demographic trends are data, and numbers do not lie. At the time, demographics were beginning to be explored professionally; however, for me, such trends were intuitive. Maybe that is one of the reasons why I used to say "I just knew" what would work at Godiva.

Chapter 8

KEYS TO THE CANDY STORE

I was a pioneer in the use of celebrity marketing. During Godiva's formative years in the '80s, associating a celebrity with a product or brand was not yet commonplace. Stars at that time did not own their own companies, they were busy working in entertainment. The era was still one in which the rare endorsement was highly compensated and often any ads appeared only overseas.

It wasn't that Hollywood agents and managers didn't want their clients to be in the limelight as much as possible. The talents' handlers preferred to spend their time booking film and television projects that brought fame, fortune, and awards.

There were also a lot fewer celebrities in the '80s and '90s. Only a few television networks existed. There were no streaming or downloading platforms on the internet. A handful of studios made only as many films as they could get financed. Personalities during that era tended to want to nurture their image.

There was an art to engaging Godiva with famous people. I learned to partner with stars on their projects, which meant a lot to them. Publicists received a lot of free chocolates every year. That's how I kept the door open. My strategy was for them to come to us. Then we said "yes" and made it seem like a tie-in was the celebrity's idea.

This method of engagement meant that Godiva got involved in supporting events that did not necessarily have anything to do with chocolate or retailing. My goal was to correlate celebrity engagement with an increase in sales. Godiva hoped to benefit from the "halo effect," meaning our product's association with an event or an appearance was expected to bring the brand positive publicity.

An example of this was when Whoopi Goldberg filmed scenes for *Sister Act* in San Francisco in 1991. During the movie's production, the catering crew had been shopping at Godiva's San Francisco Center store for desserts. There was some kind of a crew party at San Francisco Center after-hours between the time *Sister Act* was filmed and the premiere in May of 1992.

That evening, Whoopi happened to walk right into the Godiva store wearing her nun's outfit. She chit chatted with the staff; we had stayed open to supply chocolates that evening. It turns out the caterer must have been shopping for Whoopi all during the shoot because Whoopi knew the names of various Godiva pieces and clearly had her favorites. The staff packed up our largest boxes of free samples for her and had shopping bags full of Godiva Chocolates taken down to the car that was waiting to take Whoopi to her hotel.

This was happening in the Godiva store at street level while the party was going on. People were walking by the windows and taking pictures from the sidewalk of Whoopi shopping at Godiva. I was standing right there and took the photo shown on this book's website. The next day our store had free publicity all over the local news in San Francisco. It was not really planned, but Godiva had our first experience with the power of an indirect celebrity endorsement. A live, in-person star appearance gave Godiva an intangible feel-good association with a G-rated family friendly movie.

I decided this was working because it was free. The mall had hosted the party, and it didn't cost Godiva anything to offer an Oscar winner some free chocolate. I made sure that any requests that came in from studios or agents asking Godiva to underwrite events came to me. But as I soon discovered, Godiva was enough of a brand by that point that celebrities who wanted to get publicity for themselves were starting to crash our Godiva parties! (These were events paid for out of my budget in conjunction with store openings or new product launches.)

We planned a "launch party" for a new Godiva store opening at a mall in New Jersey. Woody Allen and Soon-Yi Previn (who were not yet married) came to the party and started mixing and mingling with our best customers from New Jersey that we had invited from our mailing list! The couple was clearly sending a signal to the media that they were not going to hide their relationship.

I had to figure out what was going on. A celebrity couple of such prominence would not show up at the grand opening of a pet shop or an auto parts store. My theory was carefully formulated based on thoughtful analysis of the facts. Celebrities use media to grow their own brands—their own prominence. Godiva also used media—print ads in magazines and newspapers, billboards, bus stops—to create a name for itself. Had Godiva not carefully followed me down the path towards greatness by declaring to the world that Godiva made the best chocolate, it could have faced the same fate as a hundred other chocolate brands in Belgium. Namely, it could have been just another chocolate brand from Belgium.

Advertising is a way to create awareness of a brand, whether it be a celebrity's own brand or a consumer brand. Hollywood celebrities recognized the formula Godiva was using, understanding PR and publicity as the advertising tools they are, methods to gain awareness. Hollywood stars wanted to affiliate themselves with Godiva because Godiva was successfully using the same formula Hollywood stars used in order to perpetuate fame. Godiva was getting a nod for doing things the Hollywood way and doing it well. Godiva was *respected*.

Once I figured this out, I promised myself to never stop thinking big. I will never forget the year I invited Pope John Paul II to do his Christmas shopping at our store in Brussels. Guess what—he said yes! It turns out the Pope owned his own private L-1011, a widebody jumbo jet which many airlines flew. His staff said his eminence would fly in from Rome on a certain day, and I made sure I was there and that the store looked super-stocked and camera-ready. Little did I know the Pope had his own surprise "in store" for us!

The Pope had invited two of his best friends to join him Christmas shopping—Elizabeth Taylor and her Royal Majesty Queen Paola of Belgium! There the three of them were, standing in a Godiva store, oohing and aahing over the displays.

Notice I had been careful to position Godiva as an aspirational brand, and it was paying off; royalty and heads of states were aspiring to give—and be associated with—the best, Godiva.

This taught me to avoid anyone controversial and to make sure to treat Godiva like a social climber, affiliating with kings and presidents.

In order to harness "star power" effectively, Godiva had to balance the scales in order not to be overlooked as merely a backdrop serving as a venue for a celebrity event. There had to be something in it for Godiva. I was sure to have a press release ready and a limited-edition shipment of merchandise hitting stores to accomplish retail sales momentum during media appearances.

Special events usually led to a large volume wholesale order from the studio for corporate gifts. We would print ribbon with the studio's name to tie around the ballotin. Our policy was "the bigger the order, the bigger the discount." I certainly couldn't discount in a public forum like the Godiva stores because I had shepherded the notion of Godiva as a full-price brand, meaning customers shouldn't bother waiting for a sale because there will never be one. There were no promotional discounts on Godiva during the thirteen years I managed the brand.

Actually, there was only one individual in the world who was not an employee of Godiva that had keys to one of our Godiva stores. That situation came about as a way Godiva was able to do a favor for one of our very best celebrity clients, Michael Jackson. The way that Michael Jackson, in particular, became a friend to our Topanga Plaza store is fascinating and could only happen in Hollywood.

The Jackson family compound was off Hayvenhurst Road in Sherman Oaks at the end of a long driveway lined with royal palms and sable palms. Sherman Oaks is a prestigious neighborhood in Los Angeles. The TV and movie studios of Studio City are a short ride down Riverside Drive. Beverly Hills is just over the hill past Mulholland Drive. A few exits up from Hayvenhurst off the 101Freeway is the exit to Topanga Plaza, which is built on prime real estate in Woodland Hills.

Topanga Plaza is *the* mall in Los Angeles. You are supposed to be impressed when someone says they shop at Topanga Plaza.

Anchored by Neiman-Marcus, Nordstrom, and Macy's, Topanga Plaza features vaulted glass ceilings letting California sunshine in. The breathtaking architecture is reminiscent of California's mountains and canyons—open, airy, spacious, and bright.

When Godiva's new Topanga Plaza store was announced, a general manager job posting went up on the employee bulletin board at the factory in Brussels. Séraphine was a Flemish intern at the factory preparing to graduate from the University of Leuven with a degree in merchandising. She wanted to move to California to live in her family's second home in Woodland Hills. I had known Séraphine from her work on our store design steering committee, so when she applied for the position in Los Angeles, I jumped at the chance to have her move to LA.

While we were making flight reservations, Séraphine mentioned that she would be bringing a dog, so special arrangements would have to be made with the airline. Séraphine insisted on flying KLM because their planes had a pressurized cargo hold for pets and offered a pet concierge service.

We had to fill out the paperwork. "Breed?" was the first question on the form. It turns out this puppy was a Belgian Malinois, an ancient purebred breed registered in Belgium. Malinois are extremely rare outside of the Kingdom. "Pet's Name?" came next on the form. Séraphine told me the pooch's name was "Knuffelsenkussen."

"I can't pronounce that name" I said to Séraphine. As she kept pronouncing "Knuffelsenkussen" over and over, and I kept trying to say the name properly, finally exasperated, I suggested, "Why don't we try it in English?"

"It means 'hugs and kisses,'" Séraphine told me.

"Oh, well, that's easy, why didn't you say so in the first place!", I exclaimed, realizing how cute the name is and how well it matched the dog's picture that Séraphine sent me.

That's when Séraphine told me that it wasn't her dog. She was bringing the puppy to California as a favor for her friend, Debbie Rowe, who lived in Sherman Oaks. Séraphine had made a deal with Debbie: Séraphine would safely bring the new "baby" to Los Angeles if Séraphine got to name the "baby," and whatever name Séraphine chose, Debbie had to agree to.

Séraphine felt the name was adorable, and that if Debbie's children couldn't pronounce "Knuffelsenkussen," then it would be OK with her for them to call the dog "Hugs and Kisses." Or the kids could learn to speak Flemish!

Now I began to form a clear picture of why price was no object when it came to booking flight arrangements. Debbie was sponsoring the travel. She was the ex-wife of Michael Jackson, and the dog was for their children. Debbie had been the nurse at Dr. Klein's office on Ventura Boulevard in Sherman Oaks, where Michael was a patient. That is where Debbie and Michael met. It was a true love story, according to Séraphine, who had been friends with Debbie for years. Michael was Debbie's first (and one-and-only) true love.

Fast forward to when the Topanga Plaza store opened, and Debbie came to visit. Debbie wished out loud that her children could see it. But Michael didn't want their family walking around busy places like malls in the middle of the day; he preferred privacy.

I came up with a plan. Why not give the keys to the candy store to Michael? Debbie told Michael that the mall closed at 6:00 p.m. on Sundays. By 7:00 p.m., everyone in the building would be gone, including other mall employees. Michael was invited to bring the children to the shop any time after 7:00 and let themselves in using the key. They would have the entire store to themselves without anyone to bother them. We decided on a date.

Mall security knew that a VIP would be parking on the roof of the garage and entering the building through the service corridors after hours. At closing time, the shop staff kept the lights on and the alarm off, just as if they were *not* closing, and everyone went home for the night. The chocolate case was illuminated with fifty kinds of chocolate.

I left a clipboard on the counter. Michael could write down a list of anything the children ate or took home. A bill would be "sent to the studio," which is code for "charged-off as a marketing expense," since no bills are ever sent to celebrities' studios.

When the staff arrived the next morning, the clipboard read, "10 pieces of candy. 3 chocolate covered strawberries." And there was a stack of one hundred bills on the counter! The phone rang; it was Debbie calling to thank us for the hospitality. The kids had told Debbie all about their first time visiting a chocolate store. Séraphine mentioned the pile of hundred dollar bills, and Debbie said, "Yes, that sounds like Michael. He has no concept of money. For all we know he thinks that's how much a few chocolates cost!"

Chapter 9

CONFUSION–ILLUSION–DELUSION

People outside of Godiva asked me what there was to talk about in meetings because they thought, "It's just chocolate." Wouldn't every chocolate company (or business of any type) love to have million-dollar orders arrive in the mail? Orders do not materialize out of thin air. Buyers do not wake up in the morning and think, "Today I'll place an order with Godiva." Buyers had to be presented with solid numbers summarizing Godiva's profit, so they could make the case with management to pass more orders.

On those occasions when I accompanied Godiva account executives to their appointments, I began the meeting by beaming my power point against a wall. Buyers preferred to start by going first, but too many times we let that happen, and the entire hour was taken up by the buyer talking about what they wanted (markdown money, co-op advertising dollars, priority ship dates, exclusive packaging, brand extensions, and so on) leaving Godiva no time to make our presentation! We learned our lesson in those cases when the meeting was over before we got to discuss whatever it was we came to talk about.

Buying office meetings always began with a "randomization" slide. That slide would have a column with three dollar amounts ($10, $15, and $20 million for example) and a column with three retailers' names (Abraham & Straus, Macy's, and Stern's if I was in New York, for example). The department stores' names were scrambled so as not to be shown next to their corresponding sales volume. I started each meeting saying, "These three Godiva customers' sales for last year are shown in no particular order."

The reason for randomizing was because no retailer wanted Godiva revealing their sales figures to competitors. Yet in each market our customers knew who their Godiva competition was. And I didn't care what the buyers thought, I believed the data belonged to Godiva. We were free to disseminate it.

I was literally opening every meeting with a slide demonstrating that I shared the buyer's sales figures with competitors—indirectly—and that was how things were going to be done. I was taking control.

Other slides in my power points focused on sales per square foot, penetration by door (Godiva sales expressed as a percentage of total store sales for each branch), indexing (sales breakdown by season such as "60% of sales were at Christmas"), Godiva's sales increase current year versus prior year, and Godiva category analysis (sales broken down according to chocolate, coffee, biscuits, hot cocoa, and biscotti). Godiva's account executives kept track of the raw numbers by working with their buyers throughout the year.

I talked about "money" in meetings, not "chocolate," because of my insistence on keeping the focus on profitability—profitability for the retailer, and profitability for Godiva, which kept dividends flowing directly to the shareholders. Driving up the stock price was important to have continued access to the lowest borrowing cost on Wall Street.

Godiva presentations made buyers look good to upper management. We gave buyers credit for success. When there was a rare overstock situation, Godiva took the blame. This treatment resulted in buyers often getting promoted. In retailing the sacred rule is, "the assistant always gets the job," so Godiva was attentive to assistant buyers, knowing sooner or later the assistant would become the next buyer.

Quite a few times a buyer from one retail chain left to become the buyer at another retail chain. I kept a spreadsheet to be prepared for when that happened. My spreadsheet noted details about all of our buyers. The spreadsheet came in handy when one Godiva account executive took over working with a buyer who had previously been called on by another Godiva account executive. If the spreadsheet noted that a buyer liked to be entertained, and could write re-orders up to half-a-million dollars without approval, then two things would happen. The Godiva rep taking over calling on this buyer would be sure to invite him for lunch. The Godiva rep working with his replacement buyer would write orders for about five-hundred-thousand-dollars, knowing those orders could be passed without the need for multiple approvals.

When there was industry buzz because of a major buying office change, I would ask the Godiva rep who was "at the eye of the storm" to stand up at the next Godiva meeting in order to give our group the run-down on exactly what happened by explaining how she landed the new account everybody in retailing was talking about. The salesforce loved when this happened because they got to listen to somebody besides me talk for a change. When our rep D'Arcy got Godiva into Liberty House in Hawaii, with fifty-four stores, it was considered a "coup." Godiva wanted that account but Leonidas was assumed to be the favorite and was thought to have the inside track based on their vast distribution network throughout Guam, the Northern Mariana Islands, New Caledonia, and Micronesia, all of which were areas where Godiva did not sell.

At the next Godiva conference, D'Arcy stood to address her colleagues, but her body language surprised me, as she did not merely rise at her seat, but walked confidently out to the aisle and up to the front facing the entire group. It seemed D'Arcy did not want anybody to have to turn around to listen to what she had to say! I should have known better, knowing D'Arcy. I was anticipating a treatise on professional selling. Instead, D'Arcy flung back her hair and said something like, "I had heard the former buyer was a terror. The assistant got promoted and said the previous vendor, Frango, didn't want to sell mints and other chocolates to Liberty House because of him. So...,"she looked around hesitatingly as if about to tell a secret, "when I went to the meeting and saw boxes of Leonidas samples in the office, I had to think fast and said I thought I heard that Leonidas hired the old buyer as their rep." (Liberty House would not have wanted to work with their ex-buyer calling on them as a Leonidas sales rep.)

D'Arcy giggled. I rolled my eyes. Liberty House soon went out of business, so it was much ado about nothing.

D'Arcy had originally joined Godiva as a training manager. She transferred from Vlasic Pickles just before Vlasic was spun off by Campbell's. Knowing nothing about chocolate, D'Arcy sat in on many buying office meetings but didn't have anything to add. After a few meetings D'Arcy decided the buyers needed training. D'Arcy carried a box of Godiva into each meeting, along with a binder that had pictures of all fifty flavors and fillings. D'Arcy opened the box and started describing Godiva Chocolates! News flash—buyers didn't care about what was in the box. To them it was a box of chocolate. D'Arcy soon realized we knew our audience. Buyers were only interested in financial aspects of the business arrangement. That was what made me decide to train D'Arcy as a sales rep.

If all else failed when trying for an order in a buying office meeting, I had a fallback plan. I would emphasize that Godiva was a retailer that also wholesaled. I'd show a power point I kept on a disk (the precursor to thumb drives) with pictures of dozens of Godiva boutiques. Flipping through the photos, my conversation would be about the fact that Godiva knew what retailers needed because Godiva was also a retailer! Sometimes this was all it took to convince a reluctant buyer that Godiva was not trying to "sell" them something, but that we were "partnering" on the next order we wanted signed. Buyers had limited rebuttals to this line of reasoning. Positioning Godiva as being an operator aligned with the department store—often located in the same malls—allowed buyers to think of Godiva not as a manufacturer trying to push a product, but as a retail consultant making sure the department store was going to have enough goods on hand to achieve sales plan. Plus, it was true because Godiva could not supply last-minute seasonal reorders; by Christmas time we were already producing Easter.

I could tell after calling on so many buyers that department stores were a phenomenal proving ground for people attracted to retailing careers. Department store buying offices became ground zero for recruiting Godiva sales reps. Who better to sell Godiva than people with a background as professional Godiva buyers? Mary-Margaret had bought for The Hecht Company in Baltimore, Liza worked at LS Ayres in Indianapolis, Brandy was the buyer for

Frederick & Nelson in Seattle, and SweetPea started her career at Foley's.

Foley's was based in Texas where personalities such as SweetPea behaved "large and in charge." SweetPea pushed to the limits to see if there were any limits! That gave SweetPea the type of outlook perfectly suited for a career at Godiva. Her motto was "go big or go home."

SweetPea looked the part of a newlywed Dallas rancher's wife rocking her "big Texas hair" in a typical ensemble of a fringed brown leather vest worn over a denim blouse loaded down with turquoise rings, bracelets, and necklaces.

SweetPea had married Diego Ortiz. This was back in the days when women with careers were starting the trend of keeping their maiden name after getting married. I thought if SweetPea hyphenated her maiden name, Cardiz, with her new husband's last name, her married name would be SweetPea Cardiz-Ortiz. Instead, she hyphenated her first and middle names, and became Mrs. SweetPea-Louise Ortiz. I tried to ask whether I should start calling her "SweetPea-Louise" by commenting, "SweetPea, you are the first woman I know who hyphenated her first names after getting married! Is that how your family does it?" I didn't get a verbal response; it went over her head (she waved her wedding ring at me).

I couldn't just poach talent; something had to happen. SweetPea's situation was peculiar. Bosses at Foley's told SweetPea they were "taking her checkbook away," a euphemism meaning she could not place any more Godiva orders until after Christmas. This happened in early December during a particularly important year for Godiva. Foley's had built four "test" Godiva shop-in-shops in prime locations. Sales performance was out-of-this-world. But without more stock continually arriving, the shop-in-shops kept shrinking in size because there was not enough Godiva merchandise to maintain meaningful displays in our allocated square footage near busy first floor entrances. These Godiva shop-in-shops suffered from their own success because apparently the volume caught Foley's off guard, and upper management worried that if they re-ordered, sales could abruptly stop, leaving them with bloated inventory.

SweetPea thought otherwise. Since leadership did not support her huge project, she took that as a vote of "no confidence" and came to work at Godiva.

I used to say to new Godiva reps when they first started, "It's up to you," regarding their personal selling styles. I was not going to tell reps how to call on their buyers. Godiva did not provide a "script" or employ hard-sales tactics such as imposing deadlines. I was very respectful of peoples' individual approaches. Showing up for a meeting was a performance of sorts for which salespeople needed to be "on." It was important for Godiva reps to have fun working solo out in the field. Buyers expected to be called on by a person who was a cheerleader for the Belgian chocolate industry. That was understandable because buyers spent entire workdays analyzing their Godiva business. If my reps didn't validate the buyer's hard work, who would? No one else was going to nurture those buying office relationships.

I taught my sales reps to find out what the customer was really looking for because the answer would be very revealing and was the secret to unlocking an ongoing stream of orders creating a relationship no competitor would ever be able to steal away. It took years for me to understand why other businesses didn't ask what the customer wanted. Then I finally figured out that marketing emphasizes selling what you have. *Sales is a little different than marketing*; during training I explained that Godiva didn't sell—we offered what clients needed.

One thing all Godiva sales reps had to learn was the fine art of saying "yes" even when we meant "no." Godiva's sales force understood that we had to find ways to work with people who wrote millions of dollars in orders each year. The best way of explaining it was to say that the same customer orientation and service focus Godiva upheld in our retail stores also applied to calling on wholesale buyers. The objective was for buyers to come out of every Godiva meeting feeling things were "better than before."

Godiva salespeople should not be downplayed as mere "order takers," as hard as that may be to believe. Every other chocolate company was trying to get appointments with our buyers at major chains. Godiva's reps had to work for every department store order. The high level of chocolate industry activity overall gave me an inspiration. Why couldn't Godiva salespeople branch out into being responsible for business development? We had not done much prospecting before, so I created an entirely separate rate card for commissions applicable when landing a new account. I needed Godiva reps to feel incentivized rather than realizing they were creating more work for themselves (which they were). Within a span of two years, Godiva became a part of the excitement in retailers that had never carried Godiva, such as Wegmans, Duty Free, and Barnes & Noble. We simply took a page from what other chocolate brands were doing and started copying them—namely expanding the number of customers we called on.

My only rule was that new customers had to go into the chocolate business. I would not authorize sales to a chain of coffee shops wanting to carry Café Godiva but not Godiva Chocolate, for example. I could not believe how many inquiries we received to open

Godiva Ice Cream stores. The answer was always "yes, provided your business plan calls for your ice cream stores to prominently feature a Godiva Chocolate counter." That was an example of saying "yes" when we meant "no."

Chapter 10

HOW TO EARN PROFIT FROM CHOCOLATE

As a manufacturer, it was important for Godiva not to become overly dependent on one product line or on a few major customers. If sales decreased from a particular product line or from a major retail partner, company earnings could be destabilized in the short term. That is why I believed in testing. I was continuously testing new chocolates and new retail partnerships.

Correlated to testing was the unavoidable topic of how I decided on pricing. Pricing was the first subject many retailers inquired about, because pricing conveyed quality in the chocolate business. I reexamined Godiva's approach to pricing from the standpoint of it being an important matter of mutual interest between manufacturer and retailer. The result was a modern pricing approach lending flexibility to the sales process at Godiva.

The new system I instituted, I called "custom pricing." Godiva had always used standard pricing.

Standard pricing involved publishing wholesale costs in Godiva catalogs and on Godiva order forms. All retailers paid the same price. Published pricing did not vary due to any factors. Orders large and small were billed at quoted rates. This made it extremely easy for the sales force to call on customers. It was not necessary to get a rate quote for any size order. Godiva's chocolate reps and the buyers figured out how much an order would cost using a calculator. Retailers loved standard pricing because it ensured that retailers did not compete on the basis of price. All retailers paid the same cost, sold for the same retail price, and earned the same margins. There was no fear of competitors getting a better deal. Buyers planned ahead, programming out a year's worth of orders in advance, queuing up orders in the computer ready to generate automatically since pricing was honored for one year.

At Godiva, an independent mom-and-pop chocolate shop paid the same as I. Magnin. Further, retailers knew that what they would pay was always going to be 50 percent of retail, also known as "keystone" markup. That meant when Godiva put through a price increase at retail, the wholesale cost went up to half of the new, higher retail price, meaning gross margins also increased at the same time. Standard pricing made it easy for customer service to generate invoices, as all clients paid the same price. Standard pricing was intuitive and transparent, and while some said it did not benefit higher volume accounts, another way of looking at it was to say that standard pricing motivated retailers to sell more volume if they wanted a gross margin increase.

Standard pricing eased the opening of new sales channels. Catalogs, duty-free, home shopping TV, gift basket companies, and chocolate-of-the-month clubs all had their day of reckoning up front: did they or did they not want to partner with Godiva? If the answer was "yes," then the onus fell on operators in new channels to adjust their thinking to be realistically aligned with chocolate retail margins. Standard pricing made it unnecessary for inexperienced retailers to guess or wonder what they "thought" they could charge for a product, because Godiva provided the MSRP on our rate card. At some point, goods started shipping pre-ticketed. Personally, I liked standard pricing.

Custom pricing came about as a means by which a buyer could write a proposed order as an indication of interest to explore testing some new chocolate I was working on. Custom pricing basically started out with the retail buyer preparing an order with the pricing left blank. Godiva's rep sent what was called a "pro-forma order" to the factory and waited for a quote to come back. The benefit was obvious—the retail partner was so far down the road in negotiations that they had already decided on which new chocolate to carry, what quantity to order, and the timeframe for expected delivery. For talks to have progressed to such an extent that those details had been worked out meant multiple approvals had been received up and down the chain of command. Godiva benefited from having a strong inclination that if we wanted to proceed with a test on a new chocolate at the retailer in question, in all likelihood the order would be approved if Godiva quoted pricing in line with what the buyer needed.

That meant I was departing from the "50 percent of retail" formula when pricing *new* products. I had to do it to capture business. The term "matrix" had just come onto the scene. Department store holding companies were telling each division that stores had to stock according to a "matrix." Think of drawing two crossing lines forming a four-way grid. The grid titles could be "European" low-priced chocolate, "European" high-priced chocolate, "American" low-priced chocolate, and "American" high-priced chocolate. When a buyer said he needed liquor truffles, for example, I asked the factory to make some, and we'd see what we could sell them for. In this example, the department store had money allocated to spend only in the European high-priced chocolate category. For whatever reason, the chain was not looking for American or low-priced European liquor truffles if they were talking to Godiva.

Custom pricing was designed to be nimble. It was in recognition of the fact that if Godiva did not move new products to market quickly, the department stores' only option under the matrix would be to order from another upscale Belgian brand. At Godiva, we estimated that Godiva maintained a 90 percent market share in luxury Belgian chocolate in the US, even though no third parties tracked the category. My goal was to protect market share. There were two ways to do that: introduce new products to grow top-line sales, and price effectively to prevent losing orders to competitors.

When testing Godiva using custom pricing at new retail partners, we found that reorders came in sooner than expected. Inexperienced retailers were too conservative when placing opening orders. Chocolate sold out, and we received requests to ship back-up orders sooner than expected. Previously, under standard pricing, there had been less urgency to reorder; retailers assumed Godiva had a warehouse full of inventory, so buyers felt they could pick up the phone anytime to place an order.

I was testing *pricing* just as much as I was testing new *products*. I just guessed what the prices should be. Sometimes I just made prices up! How was I supposed to know? That is why Godiva's two pricing systems supplemented each other; custom pricing never replaced standard pricing.

Tracking quotes under custom pricing required a robust back-end so that customer service was able to enter orders into the computer correctly for invoicing and billing. Custom pricing was complicated because each line on a purchase order may have had a different cost for different flavors of the same sized item. For example, Godiva quoted five costs for five flavors of new Godiva Fudge. Adding nuts increased the price. Dark chocolate required a higher percentage of expensive cocoa, so it cost more than milk chocolate. (Godiva Fudge did not pass the test phase because customers said the pieces were too small.)

But Godiva learned profound lessons about nuts during the fudge test, which led to changing Godiva recipes to better appeal to US customers. The outcome from testing Godiva Fudge was we learned that Americans prefer what Godiva came to refer to as "American nuts." The phrase refers to nuts Americans are accustomed to eating: walnuts, almonds, cashews, pecans, and pistachios. Belgian chocolates are made almost exclusively with hazelnut praline. Americans were not that interested in hazelnuts. We decided to change almost all of Godiva's recipes. I had the factory replace most hazelnuts with American nuts. Test results were unanimously favorable.

Notable introductions were the milk chocolate pecan cluster and white chocolate cashew cluster. A new almond-shaped mold had an almond inside. Half Walnut featured a walnut perched atop a chocolate shaped like half a walnut shell. The extremely talented master chocolatier developed a liquid cream that oozed out of the chocolate-shaped walnut half, an idea that was chic and trendy at the time. A triangular dark chocolate coconut piece was launched soon after. There was much discussion about whether coconut was considered a nut, but I thought it was. Fewer chocolates contained nuts at all. Godiva was at the leading edge of filling shells with chocolate of specific intensity, referring to the percentage of cocoa content. New shapes were created for dark chocolates to be filled with 72 percent dark ganache and 85 percent dark ganache.

In order to accommodate all of this testing, the hallmark of Godiva's global sales strategy was my behind-the-scenes policy of being willing to pay customs brokers to clear hundreds of *different* items through customs. Every item being imported had to be declared on what is called its own "line" on customs documents. There are fees for clearing *every* "line" on *every* order. Competitors limit their variety to reduce the number of "lines" they must pay to clear. (This customs clearance fee structure is one reason consumers often wonder why the variety in stores is becoming so limited.) Paying to clear many "lines" enabled Godiva to gather sales data from testing in our global boutiques to assure retail partners that we were offering them proven best-selling products.

It's a good thing Godiva tested because of what happened, for example, when Godiva opened a boutique in Seoul. We knew immediately a strawberry cream would have to be developed to satisfy customer demand there. A small test order shipped, but the strawberry creams got seized by Korean customs. The type of food coloring used was not allowed in Korea. That detail escaped us.

On a trip to Rio de Janeiro for a meeting with a buyer to discuss testing Godiva's new line of "mini sizes," I parked a rental car in the parking garage of what seemed like a normal area. Instead of the usual niceties, such as introducing herself or shaking hands, the woman came running out upon seeing us, a group of people in suits, waving her hands over her head in a panic. "Did you park on the street?" she shrieked practically in hysterics.

"No, we parked in the garage" I answered.

"Good," the woman responded, calming down and taking a deep breath.

I just had to ask, "Why, what would have happened if we had parked on the street?"

"The car wouldn't have been there when you went back" was her reply. What an interesting way to start a formal business meeting! I've never quite received that type of a welcome (or warning) before.

The woman was in charge of procuring chocolate for a major chain of supermarkets in Brazil and wanted Godiva to begin creating small boxes of inexpensive chocolate products to pack in gift baskets. Godiva Chocolate-covered mini-Bavarian pretzels and Godiva Chocolate-drizzled vanilla-buttered caramel corn were two ideas that resonated cross-culturally. Her idea turned out to be a good one because as the years went on, Godiva developed mini-size packages of numerous gourmet foods to add to our product line. The testing proved that even though there had previously been no such thing as Godiva chocolate-dipped pretzels, shoppers in South America did not know that we made it up just for that market.

Around this time, I recruited a new assistant. She came to Godiva from Kraft Cheese in Cincinnati. We arranged for her to start work the week I needed to make a trip to Hong Kong, so I could have an assistant with me in Asia.

The Godiva boutique in Hong Kong was testing "Limited Edition," which came about from our production orientation. Godiva sold in the US was made at the factory in Philadelphia. Godiva sold in Europe and Asia was made at the factory in Brussels. Limited Edition was the first time that chocolates made in Brussels were sold in the US. Limited Edition happened because there was excess production capacity at the Brussels factory.

"Production orientation" in business is a management state of mind which emphasizes production techniques and unit cost reduction. Manufacturers such as Godiva often focus on what they can make rather than what people need or want, which is why I was brought in as a marketer. My "marketing orientation" transformed Godiva into operating under a philosophy assuming consumers will favor those products focusing on needs and wants of our target market.

Limited Edition will only be remembered by Godiva's most devoted followers because it lasted less than six months due to the 50 percent price differential. Its distinctive packaging consisted of octagonal creamy beige boxes which we packed with paper candy cups. This was the one and only time in the history of Godiva that chocolates were "cupped" (packed in paper candy cups) rather than packed in plastic trays inside the boxes. I can't remember what Limited Edition tasted like, but I was at the factory watching them being made. It was a very hot June day in Brussels, the building was old, and it was then I realized the factory there did not have air conditioning!

Upon arrival at Godiva's Hong Kong boutique, we saw that the store's stockroom, where we would be meeting, was undergoing some construction. My assistant and I sat with the store manager and our interpreter around an oversized folding table that had been set up temporarily in the storage room. Moments later, a construction worker walked by carrying a piece of lumber, and surprised to see us, backed into the wall making a hole. The store manager told him to fix it later.

Soon a hearing-impaired salesperson came into the room carrying her cash drawer and a bank deposit bag. The store had closed.

"The construction workers have supplies piled up blocking the safe," the salesperson signed, motioning waist high with her hand, "where should I put the deposit?" The store manager translated in Chinese sign language which our interpreter translated into American sign language, so my assistant could interpret into English for me!

"No one will think of looking for it here," the manager signed, waving her hand towards her while translating for us again, which was silently interpreted from Chinese sign language to American sign language until it came out in English, sounding as if the last thing she needed to deal with in the world at that moment was more aggravation. After we passed the bank bag around the table to the manager, she reached over to the hole and dropped the bank bag down into the wall.

The saleswoman's perky, appreciative facial expression conveyed she thought that was a brilliant idea, dramatically signing, "We'll have the construction workers fish it out tomorrow." She left without even waiting for the reverse triple translation to be finished!

I considered the Hong Kong GM to be a multi-tasker. She was "a natural," who we called back then, a retail "maven," referring to a manager comfortable in their element among customers, employees, and merchandise, which are a lot of moving parts. But my assistant thought otherwise.

After this meeting, my assistant promptly quit. Her attitude was that "she couldn't handle crazy."

I still don't know whether she was referring to using the hole in the wall as a "safe," or hiring employees who couldn't talk to customers, or to zany translations (because responses sounded like they were to imaginary questions), or because test prices were all wrong (I discovered prices had been calculated backwards based on exchange rates), or all the above.

The new assistant told me she hadn't quit her other job at Kraft Cheese. She was taking a week of vacation time off from Kraft, hedging her bets to see if she would like working at Godiva. She would be going back to work on Monday in Cincinnati.

Welcome to my life! I wouldn't have it any other way.

The author at the Godiva factory, Reading, PA (near Philadelphia), circa mid-1980's

“Symphony of Chocolate,” Godiva Christmas collection, late 1980’s

Godiva outpost at a branch of Gottschalks in California, 1995 or 1996

Godiva mini-shop, late 1990's, USA

Godiva boutique, Northpoint Mall, Atlanta, late-1990's

Kelly's Coffee store, Glendale Galleria, early-2000's

Leonidas Chocolate Cafe, Sherman Oaks Fashion Square, 2009

KC Chocolatier mural, 2010's

Chapter 11

YOU'RE IN GOOD HANDS WITH ME

No study of Godiva Chocolatier's business model would be complete without a mention of the executive team I worked alongside. Believe it or not, we all worked remotely forty years ago. I must have been ahead of my time. But that meant my team did not have to interface in person very often. I barely knew some of them. Virtually the only time any colleagues would be in the same place at the same time with me (besides at conventions) was when we would have a Godiva Chocolatier store opening. Those grand openings were my opportunity to handpick someone who I needed to put in "face time" rotation, meaning we would meet in some city somewhere precisely two days before the new store's scheduled grand opening to the public.

Business managers overseeing Godiva's worldwide network of boutiques compared me with Van Gogh because the stores were like my canvas, and I handled the chocolate like an artist. People noticed I never cut the printed ribbon between the words "Godiva" and "Chocolatier," (which would separate the brand name in two) and noted my insistence on unpacking cardboard boxes in outside corridors (I could not risk bringing bugs into the store). I talked while we worked, imparting product knowledge about everything having to do with Godiva. I used to tell people, "This is what you have to know if you want to work here." I was preparing store associates for stressful days because at peak times, such as Valentine's and Easter, there would often be a line out the door.

The best part of training was when setup was far enough along that we could do role-playing exercises. I would be the customer, taking turns with each new hire serving me behind the counter, prompting salespeople on how to overcome objections from customers. My goal was to make sure there were no surprise questions that the staff did not know how to answer. It was a lot of fun because I would take on various personas reflective of the wide-ranging types of clientele likely to shop with us.

I began by posing as a "looky-loo," urging store teams not to judge a book by the cover. I'd "buy" one piece, pretend to leave the store, then pretend to return ten minutes later. My suggestion was for staff to recognize their customers with a line such as, "Look who's here—it's you!" Still posing as the faux customer, next I would say, "That piece I bought a few minutes ago was great. I'd like to buy a pound please." It happened every day in actual practice.

Another common Godiva clientele in those days were people who only set foot in a mall one time a year, during the holiday season, and were stuck in a time warp, not believing inflation could have increased prices in a year. The giveaway was those clients talked price, asking "Have the prices gone up?" or mentioning having the budget to spend only a particular dollar amount.

I would glance knowingly at the store's staff on the first day we were open for business if it was during the Christmas season when employees would meet such once-a-year visitors, remembering that we had prepared for how to serve this type of customer, during role playing. In Denver, at Cherry Creek Mall, a couple came in, and the girlfriend or wife was eyeing Godiva's bulk chocolate display longingly. The boyfriend or husband said to the girlfriend or wife, "You can get a dollar's worth!"

Without skipping a beat, the person helping the couple informed them matter-of-factly, "Godiva pieces sell for about a-dollar-fifty each." She was politely making it clear we were not standing in the penny candy aisle at Woolworth's. The boyfriend or husband was not at all offended or embarrassed. *Au contraire,* he appreciated the "news you can use" clear lines of communication. He started peppering the sales lady with questions, asking "What is the average weight?"

"Fifteen grams" she answered.

Doing the math in his head like an accountant, he said, "So that's about thirty pieces per pound," stated as a fact, not a question.

She said "Yes, we sell a prepacked thirty-piece one-pound box" motioning to the prepack wall. "But we sell individual chocolates by weight."

"How much is the one-pound box?" he asked.

"$42.50," she replied.

The man was impressed. As fast as he could fire off questions, our confident team member had the correct answers presented in a friendly way with a warm and welcoming smile. Because of the training they had received from me before the store opened, there was never any panic or "deer in the headlights" look among Godiva store staff. Their knowledge of the merchandise put customers at ease.

When we were done training in Denver, there was a blizzard, and many flights out of Denver airport were canceled. Cherry Creek happened to be about an hour's drive from my second home in Colorado Springs. Those of us from headquarters decided to wait out the storm at my place. On the drive, I outlined my vision for a new type of store I had hoped to build at either the Citadel or Chapel Hills in Colorado Springs. I wanted to develop what I called a "store without walls," which basically meant a kiosk in the mall. The format would be a prototype for smaller markets such as Colorado Springs that could not support a full-size Godiva shop. However, too many local health department ordinances caused us to put off planning a kiosk.

The day after we arrived and got settled in, I hosted a most unusual lunch for my houseguests. We loaded up provisions on several snowmobiles I kept in the garage. Getting an early start, since daylight hours are short during winter in Colorado, we rode the snowmobiles out of the back of my property, which adjoined national forestland along a mountain. On the other side of the mountain was an abandoned ghost town called, "Tin Cup."

Tin Cup had a few wooden buildings still left standing from when the area had been a gold miner's village. We set up a portable barbecue grill on the deck under the overhang of an old property and cooked hot dogs and hamburgers. For dessert I had brought Godiva chocolate bars which we melted in pans over the fire, adding milk and making hot chocolate. City dwellers from Washington DC and Boston could not imagine they would have found themselves bundled up, sitting on beach chairs, eating lunch overlooking a forest blanketed in snow high up in the mountains of Colorado that day. (I knew the bears were all hibernating for winter.)

Little did my group know that "the mountain" we happened to be snowmobiling on was Cheyenne Mountain and that NORAD headquarters was perched on top. I left that detail off on purpose because that evening I planned to entertain everyone with UFO stories. (Weird things always happened in that neighborhood, and some of my neighbors stopped by at cocktail hour to confirm that they experienced encounters similar to mine.)

Our unplanned holiday soon came to an end, and I departed to the Middle East for Godiva's next new store opening. Godiva's human resources manager joined me because we wanted paperwork to be done properly anytime Godiva entered a new nation. Godiva hired a local employment agency to handle hiring anytime we opened stores outside the United States.

Our general manager, Doug, had already been recruited. I wondered how well he would fit the organization, being an ex-Marine, because the military's mantra is "get it done," with no profit consideration. My first meeting consisted of four people: Doug, myself, Godiva's personnel director, and the person from the local staffing agency. At first, normal questions were being asked, such as Doug's address, phone number, and residency ID number. When the woman from the agency inquired as to how many wives Doug had, he replied, "Four." She wrote that down and continued on calculating the number of with-holding deductions that meant for Doug's company-provided health insurance to cover the cost of four wives.

I wanted to say, "Stop the meeting!" and ask, "Why would anyone think Doug has more than one wife? And did Doug just say he has 'four' wives?" But I was either astonished or fascinated because everyone else in the meeting seemed to think the question was expected and that "four" was a normal answer. Nobody clued me in ahead of time about the customs in this region.

As Doug and I worked that afternoon, I had to mention to him that American men ordinarily marry only one wife. Doug said that's why he preferred to live in a Muslim country. When he said that, I had a flashback to a time not long before when my Godiva account executive from San Diego told me she was quitting to move to Paris. Her reason for moving was because she "preferred to live in Western Europe." People have their preferences. Plus, as an expatriate, Doug went on to explain that he owed no taxes in the Middle East because he was not a citizen, and that he owed no taxes in Britain because his income would be under the amount exempted for citizens living abroad. So good, it worked out for him.

Doug's store turned out to be problematic in some ways at that time. We had not thought about opposition to alcohol and had to be sure not to sell any liquor chocolates. As of the writing of this manuscript, Godiva's new owners extended that decision to the entire Godiva product line, meaning all Godiva Chocolates sold worldwide no longer contain alcohol. The other factor we had to adjust for was temperature, which stayed above one hundred degrees much of the year, melting customers' purchases as people walked to their cars. We started bagging all purchases in thermal insulated bags lined with gel packs.

Soon, I looked forward to attending the Godiva store opening in uptown Albuquerque, the "store without walls" concept I had wanted to do in Colorado Springs. This time Godiva's corporate attorney was with me. He kept questioning my winning retail formula in front of the team, and I discreetly needed to let him know *I will not have it.* I had to establish the pecking order by taking him into the stockroom and saying to him at one point, "I'm not going to court to tell you how to practice law, and you're not coming to the mall to tell me how to manage a store." He never spoke to me again after the training was over. I don't think I hurt his feelings; I think he wanted to do things his way, and I wasn't interested. At that point Albuquerque was probably store number 230, and the Godiva concept was fully evolved. For some strange reason I will never understand, people liked to play "the devil's advocate" and say things to me like this attorney did: "A little disagreement is good for an organization." I took the viewpoint that their crackpot ideas were a "test" to see if I had the ability to maintain an unwavering commitment to upholding Godiva brand standards, and I passed. (Or he may have been a "plant" sent by the board to spy on me.)

In 1999, three things happened. First, I received board approval to wholesale and retail in Las Vegas. The shareholders had thought of Las Vegas as being a place where innocent people were victimized into losing all their money. I explained that the cost of gambling was budgeted by modern households as an entertainment expense. In other cities, if a couple hired a babysitter and went out to dinner, they'd spend a hundred dollars for the night. In Las Vegas, if a couple sat at the blackjack tables and gambled a hundred dollars, that was their evening's entertainment. Either way the money was spent after the night was over. People wanted to experience different forms of entertainment. So now I was ready to enter the country's largest market where Godiva still did not have any meaningful distribution. Second, in anticipation of that happening, I had already planned a budget increase to hire more sales reps. And third, I became interested in putting Godiva's name on complementary businesses and thought Las Vegas might be the place to do so.

I contacted a chocolate school in Las Vegas and asked them to post an ad on their bulletin board. A graduate student named Joe called and told me he was apprenticing to make chocolates and was enthusiastic about roasting chocolate. I told him to forget all that because if he really wanted to make money in chocolate, he needed to join Godiva and be a chocolate sales rep. Nobody I've ever spoken to has said "yes" faster than Joe; it was a "one-call close." I think he was twenty-two at the time, and he recognized this was his opportunity to grab the brass ring. (And why didn't I ever receive any applications? I was once told by a recruiting agency that "serious" sales reps discounted Godiva as a career path because they weren't going to quit working somewhere else to "take a chance.")

I had already hired Fern, who helped create chocolate recipes for Bradley Ogden's cookbook, to manage the Portland, Reno, Lake Tahoe, and Napa Valley wine country territory. Bradley had founded the Lark Creek Inn in Larkspur, California to great acclaim, going on to win two James Beard Awards for best Chef in America and best Restaurant in America. Fern invited me to dinner with Bradley one night in San Francisco. Bradley mentioned that he was hoping Fern could join him in Las Vegas for a site visit at Caesar's Palace, where he was thinking of opening a fine dining restaurant. Fern took Joe along on the trip, so she could train him.

Things suddenly got very interesting. Joe tagged along with Fern and Bradley to tour Caesar's Palace. Caesar's management asked Joe during conversation how they all knew each other. Joe explained that he and Fern had been brought on by Godiva to open a chocolate restaurant or a chocolate hotel in Las Vegas. Joe just blurted that out of his own accord without prompting! That was not bad creative thinking for the new guy on his first day on the job. Upon hearing that, Caesar's proposed that *we* get creative and open our first Godiva boutique in a hotel lobby, which we did, in Caesar's Palace, near the Forum Tower elevators.

I never forget anything (I have a photographic memory), so I had made a mental note to explore Joe's vision of possibly licensing a "Godiva hotel." I asked Joe to join me on one of my Las Vegas visits, once I was finally able to arrange a meeting with local casino mogul Mr. D. Mr. D was a regular customer at Godiva's Somerset Mall store in his hometown of Detroit. Lately Mr. D had been buying up land in Las Vegas and was building casino resorts as if he had planted seeds and watered them. My quest was to try to get Mr. D to "theme" one of his new properties as a "chocolate hotel." "Chocolates and romance," I said to Mr. D during the meeting, "What combination goes better together? Las Vegas is all about romantic getaways." I presented an entire binder filled with renderings.

At that time, Las Vegas was trying to de-theme resorts, making hotels look more like properties you could see in any world-class city. Mr. D explained how his business model was different than MGM and other casino operators. His casinos were designed and operated to earn revenues in equal amounts from each of four categories: retail, rooms, restaurants, and gaming. Mr. D sensed which way the industry was headed and wanted a diversified revenue base less dependent on gambling than other casinos were. He loved our suggestions of chocolate images on wallpapers in guest rooms, chocolates in mini-bars, and a chocolate fountain photo-op in the lobby. It could have worked out if Mr. D. hadn't had to push back his construction timetable while acquiring zoning for all the parcels of land. The delays meant starting all over again with entitlements for permits. Later, when his new casino's name was finally announced, it was called "The D Hotel." Mr. D named the resort after himself, and you can't argue with that.

As a consolation prize Mr. D. did arrange an introduction to Sheldon Adelson who was willing to take a meeting to discuss building a Godiva Chocolate theme park attraction near his Las Vegas Convention Center. I met Mr. Adelson once, at the Venetian, and do not remember him as being particularly interested in chocolate per se, but very interested in unit financial performance. Once Mr. Adelson heard Godiva's numbers (our national average sales were $1,000 per square foot), he became quite animated and what I called an "enthusiastic" landlord, so we built a Godiva store in his Grand Canal Shoppes. Within one year Godiva went from having no stores in Las Vegas, to having two stores in Las Vegas. That marked the end of expansion into new cities for Godiva in the US. From then on, new stores infilled existing US markets, and the focus pivoted to international growth.

The benefit to Godiva of continuing to operate stores in export markets to this day, is Godiva's customer service standards abroad remain so high that Godiva is one of a very few select brands the public does not seem to complain about. I cannot recall the company ever having received negative feedback from a consumer during my time at Godiva. Post-pandemic, as service standards seem to slowly slip at other premier brands, Godiva's shopping experience remains in the upper echelon alongside Tiffany and European designers.

Today Godiva's branded retail chocolate cafés are scattered across the Middle East, Asia, and Europe. Godiva's boutiques have evolved into full-service "cafés," serving beverages, pastries, and ice cream. I think people go to Godiva to relax and enjoy a break in their day, putting customers in a good mood.

Essentially, the secret to Godiva's success is that its customers feel they are "rewarded." The "reward" is that Godiva still operates a full-service chocolate store, meaning walk-in customers who make the journey to Godiva's boutiques are served without having to wait while employees answer the phone or fill mobile orders from third-party delivery apps, which simply is not done in the branches. Foot traffic takes precedence; after all, that is what a store is built for. Godiva shops did not even have telephones on the sales floor during my tenure, and that program appears to be a surviving policy of mine.

Chapter 12

DON'T CONFUSE ME WITH THE FACTS

I am also an investor. While I was working at Godiva, I accumulated shares in a chain of twenty coffee stores called Kelly's Coffee. Kelly's was based in Century City. What I liked about Kelly's was that every time I walked by, Kelly's in Century City had a huge line.

Most people outside of Los Angeles have never heard of it. But Kelly's was the originator of sweet frozen coffee drinks blended with ice and was way ahead of its time. Kelly's was part of the "first wave" of the specialty coffee craze that started in California. National coffee brands that came along later had cold drink menus that were inspired by the idea of Kelly's best-seller, chocolatey frozen blended mocha beverages that had not been discovered by mainstream America yet.

I was methodical about taking a business approach to growing Kelly's to fifty stores and winding up gaining a seat on the Board. The experience provided my coffee background, which I intended to apply at Godiva but actually put to use later at Leonidas.

My hobby, for lack of a better term, had been for years to drive around to malls on weekends and talk to Kelly's licensees. The idea of independently-owned retail shops operating as an affiliation outside a franchise model was fascinating to me. What I heard consistently in all my interviews with Kelly's owners was that the stores made money. Most Kelly's licensees wished they could own more stores! That was a good sign.

During my store visits I heard Kelly's store owners' life stories and began to understand the depths of the drama that takes place daily in major malls. Every mall has its own personality based on the neighborhood, the tenant mix, the customers, and most importantly the mall's store employees. I was inspired by the woman who was deliriously happy that she had met her husband at the mall. Another woman was touched when her father bought her a Kelly's store as a wedding present—the gift that keeps on giving.

The store in Cerritos was Kelly's number one location based on top-line gross sales. It featured a full lunch menu. The operator baked fresh bread, roasted whole turkeys, sliced the turkey, and served it on the bread as sandwiches. I had never seen anything like it. Neither had the customers who lined up every day, attracted by the aroma while walking past. But none of that would have mattered had an owner not been working at the counter. The public likes to be taken care of by an owner. Licensing the stores to owner-operators ensured profitable management! Each store owner had to be able to take enough profit out of the store to live on.

Kelly's licensees had free reign to develop new menu items such as the Cerritos lunch menu. The Cerritos owner's sister decided to open a Kelly's in Del Amo Mall. She gave me one profound lesson in retailing: *don't confuse customers with the facts. Marketing needs to give people an excuse to do what they want to do.* Everyone wants to buy a treat, so tell people their life will be better when they do.

Kelly's best-selling treat was fudge, but Kelly's stores also had a full suite of commercial bakery equipment in back of each store, including stand mixers and copper kettles used to bake on-site daily. Display cases featured caramel apples, croissants, brownies, cookies, and pastries. Coffee drinks themselves were quite elaborate because Kelly's coffees could be ordered with flavored whipped creams, caramel and chocolate drizzle sauces, and toppings such as roasted cocoa nibs and honey-coated pecan bits.

The group of licensees was entrepreneurial and found many clever ways to increase sales. When I was visiting the Carlsbad store next to a marine base, the licensee explained that he had applied for a wine and beer license. The store was next to a movie theater, and every hour, after the movies let out, hundreds of potential customers walking by were enticed in for a cold beer as a nightcap. Kelly's Glendale Galleria store owner told me she bought a pushcart, loaded it up with pump thermoses, jugs of cream, and cups and went through the mall's employee corridors early in the morning before the mall opened. She'd knock on the service doors and sell coffee and muffins to mall employees who could not leave to get coffee because they were getting ready to open. The Brentwood licensee took it a step further by starting a wholesale division to supply her fresh muffins to numerous businesses daily throughout Los Angeles.

Kelly's was an affordable concept for a first-time business owner because there were no up-front licensing fees. By adding a small profit margin to the price of coffee and other inventory, Kelly's corporate office did not have to charge monthly royalties. This was all the more amazing when you realize that Kelly's did not have its own commissary. Food ingredients were procured on the open market, meaning if a licensee wanted to price check, they could call a supplier and pose as a new customer to compare what pricing they would get by buying direct. The secret was group buying power. Kelly's corporate office was negotiating with vendors on behalf of the entire chain. In return, all shopkeepers were expected to maintain brand consistency by ordering from the same suppliers. This ensured training could be accomplished every time a new store opened, because recipes using the same ingredients would always turn out tasting the same. So, their system worked.

My plan was to market Kelly's. The only thing missing from Kelly's business equation had been marketing. Kelly's, up until the time I got involved, had strictly been an impulse purchase. A person had to be walking by one of the stores to consider making a purchase.

What happened around the time I made this realization surprised me and worried the licensees: the chain had been put up for sale! Licensees wondered about what might happen under new owners, good or bad. No one likes change or uncertainty. At that point I was more or less a known entity to people who owned Kelly's stores. They couldn't really figure out what I was doing there, basically nosing around, but I was friendly enough and always bought something, offered suggestions, and seemed at least "neutral." In retailing, that means I was not threatening. In other words, things could not get worse with me.

Soon a coalition of Kelly's Coffee licensees approached me to see if I would buy Kelly's. We went to lunch in Orange County. There was a group of at least fifteen to twenty store owners. Their proposal was for me to acquire the brand. But there was a sense of urgency because apparently a lot of bills had gone unpaid by

Kelly's current ownership group. A court hearing was scheduled for the next week to hear creditors' claims. I said during lunch that I would need to research what steps could be taken in this kind of situation, meaning, could anything happen during the hearing that could affect the sale, and, if so, what, and what could I do about it?

By the time of the Kelly's court hearing, I had determined that if the creditor's liens could be resolved by paying those bills myself I could make an argument to the court that I had effectively bought the Kelly's brand, thus avoiding bankruptcy. I showed up in court that morning in downtown Los Angeles with multiple cashiers' checks in varying denominations. I had learned that the courts expect persons offering settlements to appear in person and with cashier's checks in hand. But the problem was I didn't know how much money I'd need to spend that day. So, I stuffed my briefcase with cashiers' checks worth about $100,000!

The way it worked was that as each "tranche" or "docket" of bundled claims was presented, the judge asked if any representative from Kelly's corporate office was present to settle the "due bill/invoice." The current owner's attorney was present but acknowledged that he was representing the client only to take notes as to the outcome, not to tender funds. Each time, as a dollar amount of money owed was read into the public record, I raised my hand, approached the bench, and sorted through various denominations of cashier's checks until I had the right combination to add up to the total. A $16,000 bill could be paid with a $10,000 check plus a $5,000 check and a $1,000 check. I had them all handy.

Audible gasps were coming from the gallery, which was packed with Kelly's Coffee licensees. At one point during the proceedings, Her Honor actually stopped mid-sentence and asked for a show of hands as to how many Kelly's Coffee store owners were present. I was about to find out why!

The proceedings continued until about $75,000 in past due invoices were paid by me. The judge declared that the court could now declare the company's assets could be sold to the highest bidder. She called up any Kelly's Coffee licensees who wished to express an opinion, so they could have an opportunity to speak to the court. One by one, the licensees very briefly introduced themselves by name, stated which store location they owned and said they thought the company would be in very good hands being run by me! The judge summarized by saying she agreed, and that I had already spent $75,000 that morning, which in her opinion was more than Kelly's Coffee was worth. With that, she banged down the gavel and named me the new owner.

I took the brand from twenty stores to fifty stores in three years, which is ten new stores per year for three consecutive years—almost one new store per month if you minus out the busy Christmas season. I did this by using a contrarian marketing philosophy. I put Kelly's stores in places that had nothing to do with work. I positioned Kelly's as a fun place people would want to go to on their day off. If people go to Peet's Coffee to order a latte, so they could cozy up to their desk at work, Kelly's had to be the brand people would never associate with work. I built new stores in malls, next to movie theaters, at the beach, and near schools. Kelly's would be a place you'd want to go, not a place you'd have to go.

What no one (except me) knew at the time was the reason for my acquisition of Kelly's. My plan was to use Kelly's to learn the retail "wet coffee" business, develop popular coffee drink recipes, and experiment with retail prices, beverage sizes, and materials drink cups were made of (I chose Styrofoam). My plan was that at some point, Godiva stores were going to become chocolate cafés. Someday Kelly's would license its drink recipes to Godiva as a turn-key solution to jumpstart the transition when the time was right.

But for that to work, I had to see if Kelly's appealed to upscale clients. That meant building some Kelly's stores in malls that had a Godiva store. The aforementioned malls in Cerritos, Del Amo, Glendale, and Century City all featured both a Godiva and a Kelly's store. Suddenly it occurred to me—I had my answer, and it was staring me in the face: these Kelly's locations were top performers.

This was all happening during the very beginnings of the internet. Back in the day, Caribou Coffee's website had as their "claim to fame" a blurb saying something to the effect of, "we have 75% of our sales in the register by 10:30 a.m. every day." I knew my marketing strategy was working because Kelly's had 100% of our sales in the register after 10:30 a.m. every day! We were in malls that did not even open until 10:30!

By focusing on the sweet, chocolate-based frozen drinks, Kelly's created the afternoon coffee break rush. Our busy period was from 2:30 to 5:00, after school and "coffee break" time. I had proven by the numbers that coffee was no longer just a morning product; coffee was becoming an all-day beverage. By staying open evenings, we were leading the charge into coffee shops being a meeting place for people on dates at night during a time when other coffee shops often closed by 2:00 or shortly after lunch.

Kelly's menu featured something for everyone in the family. A group shopping at the mall could stop once, order once, and pay once. A mother with children did not need to go to Wetzel's and Dairy Queen and Gloria Jean's, interrupting her shopping time. I think this is why Kelly's wound up being number three in market share in the extremely competitive Southern California market, while being run by me, Brad, out of my home! Strong numbers made it easier to open new stores, so next I had to figure out a way to grow.

I had never sold licenses before and set about finding a way to market Kelly's to entrepreneurs. Where was I going to market Kelly's to find folks willing and able to spend a quarter million dollars to build a store? And who would be interested enough in Kelly's concept to be willing to stand behind the counter at Kelly's for the next ten-year term of their ten-year lease? The answer was at LAX! I took out small inexpensive ads near the baggage carousel or over by the taxi stand line. The appeal was to foreigners who had just landed in California intending to start a new business and make a life for themselves here. I figured anyone who flew in would be in a position to invest, might not know where to begin, and kind of had to hurry because they'd need the business to support them.

I would get calls from the airport all the time. Someone would say they had just arrived and were interested in hearing about opening a Kelly's store. I'd arrange to meet them at Century City, so they could sit and watch the amount of business being done while we enjoyed a cup of coffee and talked about America. My homework assignment was to have the applicants drive around to shop a few Kelly's stores, and as part of their due diligence, talk with as many Kelly's owners as they could.

I knew which mall landlords would accept a cash security deposit in lieu of looking at someone's credit score or net worth. I kept a waiting list, and when a new licensee's name moved to the top of the list, they were assigned to whatever store location became available next. There was only one time when I skipped someone to the head of the line. My friend Misty got Northridge, which was the store everybody wanted, because she was the chocolate buyer at Macy's. Misty was doing the same thing I was: diversifying for the future. Misty had written tens of millions of dollars' worth of Godiva orders, so she could have whatever mall she wanted for her Kelly's.

It was during this period of rapid growth that I took another chapter out of Godiva's playbook. I convinced Justin, by far my preferred contractor, to be the exclusive Kelly's contractor. Justin and his brother, who owned a cabinet shop, developed a modular interior décor package that could be assembled on-site in record time. Justin always had a few store "kits" ready to go on a moment's notice. As soon as a lease was signed, Justin would prepare the site and drop in the fixturing so fast the landlord often didn't even know we were open. This system was similar to the way Godiva's national contractor in Nashville prefabricated Godiva countertops and cabinetry to be dropped into place on-site.

Justin decided to become a co-investor of sorts. He would sign Kelly's leases, build each store, operate them for a month or two, and when my phone rang from LAX, he would sell the fully functioning turnkey shop to the licensee. Justin had strong financials and was able to secure the leases. My planning for growth was focused on eliminating bottlenecks. Opening stores on spec with Justin avoided the issue of licensees having to qualify financially. *Kelly's was a sure thing.*

So that became Kelly's marketing slogan at retail. "When you want a sure thing" appeared as the tag line next to a photo of our chocolate frozen coffee drink on posters in stores. We also used pop-up tents, which are tri-fold table toppers in the mall's common seating areas. Customers were telling us that we made the drinks right, the first time, every time. Shoppers in a hurry came to know Kelly's as a place where the line would keep moving, and they could order with confidence because their drink would be made right. It was as simple as that. There was no magic formula to Kelly's other than doing what we did every day for a price about 30 percent lower than competitors. But we never competed on the basis of price.

Then the day came when I was made an offer I could not refuse for Kelly's. The buyer—a multi-national conglomerate that had partnered with us on co-branded test stores—was only interested in acquiring Kelly's on the condition that I take a seat on the board as a strategic advisor. Feeling flattered, I said that was fine with me. I'd get paid for my opinion and could help grow "my baby." I remained the majority, minority shareholder, meaning I held more ownership shares than any party other than the controlling stakeholder.

The new ownership's first big change was filing paperwork in Washington, DC, for Kelly's to become a franchise. This necessitated spending $50,000 in legal fees in order to draw up the application. I voiced my objection to franchising because legal expenses were going to have to be recouped by charging store owners franchise fees. Doing so would erode store profits. In cases when a Kelly's owner wanted to sell their store, the books needed to look as good as possible. The board did not realize that a strong secondary market existed for Kelly's stores. A unique differentiator of the Kelly's system was that many of my first-time owners were building stores to flip them for a profit rather than holding on to them as operators. I felt franchising would make it harder to sell Kelly's stores in the secondary market, slowing down unit growth.

Soon the new ownership decided to change my long-standing policy of grandfathering in existing licensing contracts. Rules that had been in place when I acquired Kelly's, had stayed in place. I honored all pre-existing agreements and policies. Things were done my way for a reason. I needed the core group of twenty owners to speak highly of their experience with Kelly's. That way when people thinking of opening a Kelly's checked around, they heard good things. And it worked. Of the thirty stores I opened, twenty-four were owned by new operators. But that all changed once former licensees were transitioned to franchise documents. For example, I was no longer able to offer a new site to the core group of twenty Kelly's owners on a preferential basis.

Next the new owners started chipping away at my branding. To save money on printing and to avoid print minimums, paper products such as cups, napkins, and sugar packets would no longer feature Kelly's logo. It became obvious to me at that point that I was dealing with a company that had always been a manufacturer and was inexperienced in retailing. The new owners did not understand the basic principle of retail marketing is to brand anything!

Part of the conversation about branding was an announcement that posters and advertising used for in-store marketing would no longer be provided free as I had done. Franchisees were told they would have to pay for posters and menu board inserts. Store owners were told this change was necessary because of the high costs of designing, printing, and shipping that Kelly's corporate office was incurring. But that was not what was really happening. The new ownership group had secretly begun charging vendors a "referral fee" for permission to use Kelly's store list to contact franchisees. Thus, vendors were underwriting the full cost of producing in-store advertising.

I did use my powers of persuasion to get the board to understand that it would appear to store owners that what corporate was doing was pushing down marketing costs to the store level.

But my warnings were too little too late because of course, a small community of like-minded store owners who had known each other and their vendors for decades cannot keep secrets. As franchisees were calling vendors to place weekly orders, they would complain about how terrible the new ownership was for charging for something that I had always provided for free. Vendors were quick to say that didn't make sense because vendors were the ones now being asked to pay for the advertising. As I predicted, franchisees felt the new ownership was double-dipping by charging both stores and vendors for these advertising costs.

Fireworks started to fly once the new owners had been caught doing a no-no, and eventually Kelly's fell apart. I like to think of it as being a case of "all good things must come to an end." Today there is only one Kelly's remaining, which is Justin's store in Beverly Hills. My belief is that the new owners simply did not know what to do with Kelly's. It was too big to be run as a small business by me, but it was too small to be run as a big business by them. What I would have liked to have seen would have been for the franchisees to have been given the brand to manage as a co-op. As a group of entrepreneurs, that might have worked. But I was out-voted.

The "dividend" that I got from owing Kelly's was that it was an incubator for my marketing ideas, and love them or hate them, I put my money where my mouth was and paid to play. Investing in Kelly's as a side project brought out an entrepreneurial side to my marketing schtick. My experience at Kelly's taught me that the future is bright. People with skills have options, and my services will always be in demand.

I had begun to think about what might happen if Godiva was ever sold, and new owners decided to bring in their own management team. For the first time I considered potentially owning and operating my own brand rather than managing someone else's brand. Who knew at that point what the future might bring? As it turns out, lessons learned during the Kelly's saga were about to be applied at a global brand much sooner than I had ever anticipated.

Chapter 13

STANDING IN THE HALLWAY IN BRUSSELS ONE DAY

"If chocolates could talk, they'd want to be enjoyed as a daily indulgence paired with a good cup of coffee." That was exactly my pitch to the headhunter representing the investors who owned Leonidas, an upscale Belgian chocolate brand operating 1,500 locations worldwide. This is the story of my transition to CEO of Leonidas US. I developed the "chocolate café" store prototype in Brussels in order to expand the format worldwide, including US stores in Los Angeles, Chicago, and New York.

The situation unfolded when I received a telephone call from my agent Brennan, who was a partner at the premier business representation agency in Beverly Hills. Brennan was on the lookout for chocolate companies where I might find a soft landing in the event Godiva sold. I had told Brennan that the Leonidas board had always said there was a job waiting for me at Leonidas. Since Brennan knew I would be attending a trade show in Belgium, he arranged for me to take a meeting with the headhunter who formally appraised potential candidates on behalf of Leonidas.

The headhunter and I met at the Le Meridien Hotel in Brussels. He wanted to remain incognito, without getting noticed, working out of some unassuming conference rooms to avoid unnecessary attention. When I arrived at a fourth-floor board room, and we started talking, suddenly there was a knock on the door. I jumped up, not wanting to be seen interviewing in case I had been followed. I hid around a corner, out of sight, while the headhunter cracked open the door. He spoke to someone for a moment, and the door closed.

We decided I should gather my briefcase, take the elevator back down to the lobby, and then come up a different elevator to another conference room the headhunter had reserved on the third floor. Upon reaching the lobby, I saw a lot of people I knew from the show. It dawned on me that other executives might have been setting up interviews with the headhunter.

Thinking fast, I said hello, told people I was staying at the Le Meridien, and excused myself to go back to the elevators. Getting off on the third floor, I could not remember the number of the conference room the headhunter had given me. There weren't that many to choose from, so I knocked on a door. Nobody was there, but a door down the hall opened—the headhunter had been waiting and heard me knocking on the wrong door. He waved me over and closed the door.

Inside the room, the Le Meridien's loden décor of Scandinavian hunting lodge antiques in a neutral palette featured two delicate chairs with legs made from reindeer antlers and seats upholstered in burlap or scratchy material like it. Both chairs were centered facing each other on an area rug defining a seating area with nothing more. The set-up reminded me of a TV interview. The headhunter sat down in one of the two chairs and asked me to take a seat.

Not wanting to sit down yet, because the antique chair looked so uncomfortable, and while motioning to the empty seat, I hesitated before asking, "May I sit in this chair?"

"That's what it was made for," he smirked, adding after a two-beat pause for effect, "in the same century when Leonidas was founded."

I undid the button on my suit jacket. As I slowly began to sit down, the chair made creaking noises, so I stopped and stood back up. I picked the chair up off the ground and moved it over a little bit, setting it back down on the rug to make sure it was stable.

The headhunter silently watched. I sat down a second time, realizing the chair back was made of uncomfortable pieces of wood. So, I scooted forward and sat perched on the edge of the chair.

Seeming satisfied that he had placed me in "the hot seat," the headhunter proceeded to say that he had not bothered to ask Brennan for my vitae because so many people on the Leonidas board felt that my reputation preceded me. "As you know, we have the CEO position open in North America," he said, "so tell me about what Leonidas would look like under your direction."

After reminding him of my background, I spent an hour discussing my vision for the future of chocolate: retail chocolate cafés. Mostly I felt the time had come; I was qualified to be a CEO. Leonidas was appealing to me because Leonidas was on the precipice of something great. I remember saying that "I knew how to put Leonidas on the map." My closing remark was to ask for a meeting with the shareholders. Ever the salesperson, I was advocating on my own behalf.

It is important to understand that Leonidas is a household name in Europe to the same extent that Hershey's is a household name in the US. The chance to meet with the co-owners would be a momentous event because the three of them rarely convened, doing so only when necessary to shepherd their asset.

There was no hesitation as the headhunter briefed me about Leonidas's ownership structure in such a way that made it clear I was under serious consideration. I felt as if I had accomplished all that I had come to do at the show that week in Brussels, so a date and time were arranged for a meeting in Monaco.

I was given an address in Monte Carlo. The instructions were to go in the front and then go out the back. But in order to do that, I was told I would need to locate my three favorite Leonidas Chocolates and rotate the trays they sat on according to a particular sequence to unlock the back door. Once outside, I was told to cross a large private courtyard and look for a topiary as my landmark.

When I arrived at the address I was given, it looked like a Leonidas store. I thought it was a store. Maybe it wasn't a store. Nowhere in the world have I ever encountered a chocolate store with a pad on the ground at the entrance to step on to open sliding doors automatically, like at a supermarket.

This seemed like a strange part of Monaco to open a store in. It was down by the wharf. Punctuating most blocks of centuries-old townhouses overlooking the water was at least one ultra-modern glass façade building with an office appearance. Could this dark storefront have been a mirage? I wondered to myself whether a temporary replica of a store was being built as a movie set, perhaps to film a TV commercial.

Multiple security cameras were making "whirring" noises as the cameras' eyes were rotating to follow my movement on the sidewalk. When I stepped on the pad built into the sidewalk at the door, the opaque sliding glass panels on the storefront changed color from black to clear on the storefront. Looking inside, I saw no customers. To the left was a chocolate counter at least fifteen feet long.

Suddenly I could hear a voice talking through an intercom from overhead, saying "Shop at your own risk." The sliding door panels moved left and right, so I entered. There were no employees inside. Individual pieces of chocolates were displayed on seven-inch square flat gold metal trays. Row after row of each flavor of chocolate were lined up like soldiers on each tray.

Positioning myself behind the counter, without lifting anything, I shifted the tray of Alexander le Grand (dark salt caramels) a quarter turn to the right. Next, I located Eve (dark vanilla buttercream) and shifted that tray a half turn to the left. Silently I scanned the case and found Africa (dark chocolate ganache truffles) and swiveled that tray a three-quarter turn to the right. Instantly the glass French doors leading to the patio at the rear of the store swung open. As I suspected, certain chocolates trays were sitting on weights. I had been given a combination to dial, like working a bicycle lock, based on my three favorite chocolates I had been asked about during the interview. The combination was twenty-five degrees to the right, fifty degrees to the left, and seventy-five degrees to the right.

I exited the long narrow store, which measured no more than 500 square feet, and confidently crossed the luxuriously appointed "outdoor room" set up on the 2,000-square-foot patio. On the far side of the patio was a spiral potted topiary six feet high. What I was told would be a video screen could easily have been simple two-way glass.

"Five, four, three, two, one, *the chilly wind blows over the snowy plane*, one, two, three, four, five." I stated the phrase I had been given out loud, counting down before and counting up after, CIA-style.

(Someone I told this story to later said that is a famous line from an old movie.) I felt as if I had stepped out of the real world and become a character in a fantastical gaslight scene from someone else's alternate reality. But in my mind, I knew this was all really necessary for security reasons. Then a hidden panel on the ground floor of the side of the courtyard magically opened.

When I walked in, I was standing in what could have been mistaken for the elevator foyer of a museum of priceless antiquities or the entry hall of a palace belonging to Flemish royalty. "You are right on time," the butler said as he appeared out of nowhere and then led me to a glass elevator. Upon pushing the single "sea level" button, which consisted of a fingertip recognition scanner, the elevator began to lower.

We emerged on a private enclosed pier. The dock had a covered ceiling but only three walls, leaving one side completely open to the water, offering views of the Mediterranean on a beautiful sunny summer day. From the quay I climbed aboard a waiting tender with a captain who sailed us out to what I soon realized was a 250-foot mega-yacht anchored in the harbor.

As the tender pulled up alongside a deck that had been lowered from the yacht into the sea, I was helped aboard by the bosun. With a friendly welcome from a purser, I was shown to a stairway. The yacht railings were all made of glass, which projected a contemporary look, with chrome and mirror accents everywhere. The trio I had come to meet were relaxing on the upper deck on sumptuous purple velvet sofas in a sort of covered indoor-outdoor salon with walls of windows that slid open on tracks. Standing up, they greeted me warmly and introduced themselves.

Madame Iona was from Athens. Looking like a glamorous movie star, her late father had founded the company, and Leonidas still used his secret recipes. She wore an orange flowy dress and unique eyeglasses made with wooden frames, something I had never seen before. Her gregarious personality was what I expected from a person who doesn't have a care in the world.

The younger two co-owners were cousins, a man from Mykonos, Orion, and a woman from Monaco, Solaria. Both appeared to be in their mid-twenties. Orion was tan and had a full head of brunette hair (as Greek men are known for). He had on shorts, a shirt with not very many buttons, and Topsiders with no socks. Solaria wore her blond hair up in an "I Dream of Jeannie" bun, and in her clear plastic high- heeled sandals, she was as tall as me. Solaria's outfit was a two-piece white skirt and blouse cut on the bias to present a unique silhouette, accented with lightweight shell-shaped buttons.

Hors-d'oeuvres, canapés, and drinks were served, and we spent hours talking about everything and anything other than their business. It was clear the shareholders wanted to get to know the person who they were considering to run their North American division. Orion did not speak English, so our conversation had to be translated into Greek. I remember mentioning having worked at Bloomingdale's, and Madame Iona regaling us with the story of how she used to charter the Concorde to New York to do her Christmas shopping at Bloomingdale's.

The family favored Europe. They considered the US to be nothing but a hinterland. "We'll show you how it's done," Madame Iona said, meaning in the context of our conversation, Leonidas would demonstrate to an American how *real* money was made. Apparently, from their standpoint, "serious money" only existed in Europe. (I will agree that until I worked for the Greeks, I never knew that much money existed. After my first year with Leonidas, looking back in hindsight, I realized I had been kept on a short leash at Godiva, financially speaking.)

The trio talked politics a lot and said they thought life was better in parliamentary republics—like Greece—or in constitutional monarchies—like Monaco—but felt sorry for "scrappy" Americans living under pure capitalism who had to pay for their own health care and university educations. I just smiled and nodded politely the way one does during a cocktail party, pondering what it would be like to work for these three.

I knew enough about social niceties to make my exit when the time was right, mentioning that I had a home in Nice and would be spending the rest of summer in the South of France. Nice and Monaco are ten minutes apart by train along an open frontier, and I told them I swam every other day in Monaco's salt-water competition lap pool. I think that was what convinced them I had good taste—I was almost living their lifestyle.

The French-speaking purser wearing a Leonidas uniform like the ones worn at the factory in Belgium escorted me downstairs to the launch platform, so I could board the tender in crystal blue water on calm seas. Five minutes later arriving back at port, a car and driver were there waiting for me. When I got in the back seat, a gift, an exquisitely wrapped box of Leonidas Chocolates, had my name on it. The note attached to it said simply, "Welcome aboard!" This meant the family had agreed to my rate negotiated by my agent.

As the car started to weave through the cobblestone streets back to the train station, we drove past the street where I had entered. I looked out the window, and the Leonidas storefront was gone!

As soon as I took the reins at Leonidas a month later, I realized that the corporate culture was much different than at Godiva.

Fundamentally, executives at Leonidas, being based in Belgium, had a Western European outlook. Despite Godiva's presence in the Kingdom, Godiva had been my entirely American creation.

I attributed a second reason for my observation about the inherent differences as being due to the way privately-owned companies operate versus publicly-traded companies. At that time, Leonidas was owned by second-generation shareholders who viewed business situations through a different lens than founding members would have. Leonidas's shareholders *could* and *did* make decisions under intense pressure due to compelling high-stakes dynamics because they felt there were no wrong choices. Leonidas shareholders could not be accused of suffering from the "paralysis by analysis" mentality of overanalyzing details.

The way outcomes resulting from those impulsive decisions were perceived, depended on individual perspectives which were shaped by European cultural influences. Sometimes the Greek viewpoint flourished, meaning the owners' attitude was to treat cash flow like a river, with expenses flowing away while income replenished the flow up-stream. In other circumstances the Monte Carlo-style opinion reigned, whereby money was treated metaphorically like a lake, a fixed asset to be nurtured and protected, because there might not ever be a way to replenish dwindling reserves.

While I was running the American division, Leonidas's three shareholders couldn't stop profits from being generated no matter how much they tried to get in my way. Whenever a decision had to be made, it was a matter of which shareholders I needed to convince to do things my way; because the company voting was structured two versus one, majority ruled.

Sometimes it seemed like my primary job description was to massage the shareholders' egos, so no one would ever feel bad about losing a vote, which inevitably happened. Knowing the family had become accustomed to living off their quarterly dividends for decades, sometimes I would send out quarterly reports showing the contribution of dividend payments being generated from US operations.

The flow of information was one-way; I never heard back because in practice, I still had to answer to a crazy board made up of relatives of theirs. It is the board members who ultimately green-light production of which chocolates the public will taste. My supporters on the Leonidas board were Aunt Astrid, who considered me to be an internationally renowned authority on chocolate, cousin Thibault—hard-driving and fiercely ambitious—who believed there was no shame in losing, and grandfather Athanasios, who said my results speak for themselves. More neutral board members were Vassilis—formerly the children's regent (who had controlled Leonidas while the shareholders were minors)—best described as a fussbudget, "can't be bothered" Stavros, a late shareholder's stepson, and a great nephew, Xander (from the Daskalides side of the family, which had split off), who I considered to be a cretin for telling me I "wasn't his first choice."

(The history of what took place between the Daskalides and Leonidas families is like a Greek tragedy. I know what happened, yet both sides will deny it. Daskalides Chocolate is still widely available throughout Europe. Both families leave each other alone.)

A month after I started, a representative from the board of directors called from headquarters. I was needed in Brussels for an important meeting with all the country heads to plan for Christmas. Since there were no nonstop flights to Brussels from

California, I flew to Paris and took the Thalys train to Brussels Midi station and then rode the subway to the King Baudouin subway stop. An escalator there brought riders up to the street in front of the Anheuser-Busch tower, and to the left a half-block down was the Leonidas factory.

At the visitor entrance of the Leonidas factory was a small reception area. On the wall facing the entrance doors were two-way mirrors. Similar to a doctor's office lobby, the receptionist was able to see visitors arrive and would slide open one of the mirrored windows to offer a clipboard where guests signed in and were then given visitor badges.

As an executive, I had an ID badge and my own key code to open the security door to the left of the wall with the mirrored windows. As I made my way down the hall, pulling my wheeled carry-on luggage behind me, a woman who had been sitting behind the mirrored glass opened the door of her little office and called out, "Bonjour!" She had been on the lookout for me, it seemed!

She was Signe, the switchboard operator. I noted her impeccable style sense, which all Flemish have.

The first words out of Signe's mouth were, "I've been trying to reach you!"

"I've been on a flight," I answered.

"Yes, we know," Signe said. "I was trying to get in touch to let you know the meeting has been canceled."

"Well, thank you for letting me know," I responded, trying to hide my bewilderment, continuing without missing a beat by spontaneously adding, "since I won't be needed, I'll just be leaving," while literally making a U-turn in the wide hallway, pulling my wheeled luggage behind me.

"Great seeing you, Signe, and I appreciate you telling me the update . . . ." I tried to say, feeling ignored and not knowing whether she had actually heard me as Signe dashed back into the switchboard office as if to hastily retreat for some unknown reason.

The sound of footsteps coming down a stairway to the time clock mounted inside the security door was Signe's alert, instinctively sensing it must be someone from the executive suite coming down to go to lunch. Sure enough, Eric, the chairman, was clocking out, as required by the board. The board required the chairman to use the time clock!

"Eric, hello, I'm glad I bumped into you," I said in English. Eric greeted me, and we shook hands. "I've decided to spend €25,000 in extra marketing budget to hire Christmas demonstrators for the US stores. I'll submit a wire transfer form to accounting and email it this afternoon...."

Eric interrupted, "We don't have the budget for that! Don't bother—we could *never* afford that!"

And with that he left. Eric got in his car parked out front and drove away. Eric offered no explanation as to why the meeting was canceled, or whether there ever was a meeting in the first place to begin with. *Eric never asked what I was doing standing in the hallway in Brussels that day.*

I had come up with the €25,000 number on the spot because that was the amount of money the company had just spent on my travel expenses for the impromptu trip. This episode was so typical of Leonidas. There was never any discussion about costs as long as the reasons for spending money were the board's idea in Belgium. When I wanted a budget for something, I had to submit formal proposals to the board. That is why I learned to roll up U.S. expenses for packaging design, store construction, research and development, and advertising into the global expense fund administered out of Leonidas S.A. in Brussels.

Since I had made the trip to Europe, I decided to set up some further appointments. Arrangements were made for a factory tour. Fresh in my mind was the bizarre headhunter interview and trip to Monte Carlo I had to navigate to meet the shareholders. Similar smoke-and-mirrors seemed to be going on in front of me at the factory. The areas I was shown were far too clean and looked barely used for a factory that was ninety years old. I also saw a lot of mysterious unpacking of bulk chocolate going on, making me wonder if chocolate was in fact being produced elsewhere and delivered there for stocking in the warehouse.

I made mental notes that I do not have answers for to this day. But I was not responsible for production. Those questions would have to wait. I wondered what other forms of "kabuki theater" I might encounter out in the field while conducting store checks.

A guide was provided to take me to visit stores. We went to the obvious Leonidas flagship doors on Rue de Beurre, Rue des Tongres, and Rue Neuve. But I noticed many subway stations prominently featured a Leonidas shop, and they were busy. I decided to stay another day and ride the subway around town alone, winding up way out in the suburbs. Exiting the subway car and crossing the tracks, I spotted the familiar Leonidas illuminated signage at the station I was in.

As I approached and looked closer, I was horrified to see that the licensee had simply lifted the plastic shipping trays used to transport chocolates from the factory, out of the cardboard shipping cartons, and set the plastic trays down on the chocolate counter. Luxury chocolates were being displayed in brown plastic shipping trays on the sales floor. It was by far the worst display I have ever seen at any chocolate store operated by any chocolate brand anywhere in the world.

I showed my corporate ID to the three young salesclerks, speaking to them in English. They were clearly surprised that I was there and expected everyone from the company to be on vacation.

All three eagerly proceeded to ask if they could be of assistance. Somewhat facetiously, I expressed surprise that the payroll budget justified three employees working during the slowest month of the year, not sure if any of them was a daughter of the owner who might actually know how the schedule was written.

In their charming Flemish way, one of the women said, hesitatingly in English, "We are, how do you say it…riding the clock…is that what you Americans call it when we make our paychecks bigger?"

Such chutzpah! They knew from my accent that I was American. Like many Belgians, these staff were calling it like they see it and were not going to sugar-coat reality for me or for anybody.

We spent about ten minutes reviewing numerous other shenanigans their district manager "encouraged," such as leaving chocolates in the shipping trays to save on labor cost associated with transferring thousands of pieces of chocolate onto gold trays every week. I made notes, bid them adieu, and on my plane ride home, was inspired while thinking about this visit to come up with a new phrase, which I incorporated into the training manual: "sales prevention."

"Sales prevention" came to mean a term referring to unnecessary policies I could do away with because such procedures blocked sales or in some way inhibited customers from buying chocolates. I became determined to remove friction points in operations that are sometimes referred to as "moments of truth" in retail. Moments of truth are points at which consumers interact with a brick-and-mortar store, beginning at the time a customer observes the visual presentation and decides to enter, through to the way shoppers navigate the store, interact with brand ambassadors, and review signage and displays to make a purchase decision (or not), hopefully ending with an interaction at the cash register.

Leonidas expected new customers to invest the time educating themselves on *chocolates* to pack a box, versus Godiva, which built a business around choosing between types of *packaging* because boxes were already packed.

I began to form the belief that part of my legacy at Leonidas would be streamlining and simplifying procedures to get customers in and out with what they wanted while communicating the DNA of the brand effectively to each and every employee. Displaying chocolates on gold trays was what we did. As far as I know, that problem was solved. My responsibility was only to manage the Caribbean, Canada, and the U.S., so as I liked to say whenever there were problems in Brussels, "*That* happened in Belgium."

Chapter 14

THE SHOCKING TAKEOVER OF GODIVA

Godiva's marketing cast a wide net and caused a halo effect. Besides the direct impact marketing was having on sales, marketing also indirectly created an aura associated with Godiva in the public's consciousness. Often referred to as having a high "noise level," Godiva punched above its weight. Godiva's marketing campaigns "reached out and touched someone" in 1995, when one tycoon in particular took notice of Godiva, which, unbeknownst to me, is when the foundation for the eventual sale of Godiva may have unknowingly begun.

Godiva had an account, Pierre LaFond, in Montecito, near this business magnate's home, where he could have seen Godiva's displays. That is why I think the untold story of Godiva's 2008 takeover attempt started unfolding in Montecito in 1995, thirteen years earlier.

It all started the day I got a phone call from an advance woman. She introduced herself as a representative of Dr. Cherng in Santa Barbara. Her purpose for calling was to set up a meeting in person to speak on a top-to-top basis about what she described as "the view from 30,000 feet." How did she get my number? Who was Dr. Cherng? There were more questions than answers.

It was a fairly typical practice on the country club circuit to employ an advance woman to do the talking on a mogul's behalf, taking meetings as fact-finding missions to explore potential business opportunities. I had seen this type of thing done before and knew it was normal.

I agreed to meet, so one day I drove from my home in Santa Monica to Montecito, where we met at Pierre LaFond Market. The two of us were seated at a corner table talking over coffee. I'd describe her as a brunette, possibly in her late twenties, very well dressed, who I could tell was extremely intelligent and articulate.

She got right to the point, "Dr. Cherng would like to acquire Godiva."

This was serious. My first reaction was that I was glad I had agreed to meet, and relatively quickly.

"To the best of my knowledge," I went on to say, "I do not believe Godiva is for sale. However, that being said, the shareholders have indicated that I should bring them all offers whenever a proposal might unexpectedly come our way."

She requested details about Godiva's ownership structure. I summarized by saying that Class A shares were lower priced and paid dividends but had no voting rights. Class B shares were higher priced and did have voting rights. Sixty-six percent of Class B shares were controlled by the founding family. This effectively meant that no matter how many millions of shareholders there are, the family can outvote everyone and has the final say on each and every single matter, including whether to sell.

Further, whenever additional funds are needed, being a publicly traded company, Godiva could sell more shares. But such shares would always be Class A shares. The ownership percentage never dilutes. Selling shares means taking blank pieces of paper and printing them up as stock certificates. Being publicly traded on the New York Stock Exchange is like having a printing press in the basement, to print money.

The woman emphasized, "Dr. Cherng has sufficient cash on hand, and we would not be talking today if he was not serious about negotiating a purchase price for the brand."

When I asked her what it was about Godiva that Dr. Cherng was attracted to, she instantaneously volunteered, "It's scalable." She explained that Dr. Cherng wanted to own a national brand, and he wanted to own it now. The woman explained that it was her duty to help him acquire a business capable of creating generational wealth, "the gift that keeps on giving," she said, "the goose that lays the golden eggs."

We agreed that I would follow up with her after some discussions took place on my end. As I predicted, our internal Godiva conversation didn't take long. My key team felt that the journey into chocolate stardom had just begun, and that we were in business for the long haul. Godiva was going to become a global brand under my watch. My job was to report back to the woman in Santa Barbara, to communicate that we must decline Dr. Cherng's kind offer.

That follow-up phone call was brief. Our answer did not surprise Dr. Cherng's representative. "We wanted to try," she said, "because Dr. Cherng so admires the way Godiva has created a pathway to industry-leading gross margins with relatively minimal capital investment outlay."

I knew what she meant: stores don't cost that much to build, and chocolate doesn't cost that much to manufacture; as a result, each store built recouped its construction cost in two years.

A couple of years later I decided to follow-up and called her to see if Dr. Cherng had invested in anything.

She remembered me, and I immediately asked, "I'm so curious, what did Dr. Cherng decide to do?"

I will never forget her answer: "Dr. Cherng's son owns a Chinese restaurant in Orange County. We have adapted his recipes for use in a completely new type of quick-service restaurant format. Guests order in a line, pay, and sit down to eat, or they may take out. All the food is healthy and freshly prepared throughout the day using only the finest quality ingredients."

Being a huge fan of entrepreneurs in general, but particularly of people obsessed with retail, I just had to say, "Congratulations! That is so exciting! I can't wait to try it. I travel a lot and will keep my eye out. What's it called?" I asked.

"Panda Express," she deadpanned matter-of-factly.

I have told this story a hundred times and will tell it another hundred times. It is a story about people who do what they say they are going to do. Dr. Cherng was bound and determined to launch a national chain, and he did it. I was told that Dr. Cherng researched that there was no national Chinese restaurant brand at the time. Dr. Cherng pioneered the now-familiar "fast-casual" restaurant format, which had not existed before.

Today Panda Express has 2,200 locations worldwide. The company is headquartered in Rosemead, in Los Angeles County. Its market cap, though, remains slightly behind Godiva.

One thing I have thought about many times over the years is whether the woman I met really worked for Dr. Cherng? After all I never met him, and I never talked to him. I think the answer is yes, the situation really happened the way his advance woman described it because the Panda Express website now references Dr. Cherng's name. And the timeline of when Panda Express started its national roll-out fits the dates. But the clincher is that *he will get in touch again later*. Little did we know Dr. Cherng's pursuit of Godiva was not going to end here; it merely paused for thirteen years.

Meanwhile, Starbucks started its investment arm Mavron. Mavron had been seeded by Howard Schultz as a way of incubating future retail giants. Over the years, Mavron bought La Boulange Bakery in San Francisco, PotBelly Sandwiches in Chicago, Seattle's Best Coffee in Seattle, and Teavana, a national mall-based tea retailer.

There was a neighborhood in Seattle where Starbucks built prototype stores for these concepts. Each became an industry leader and went national, or didn't, in which case the concept wasn't scalable, and the division was closed. Either way, Starbucks gained valuable information from each acquisition nonetheless, be it in regard to recipes, distribution logistics, IT systems, or trademarks and other valuable intellectual property.

During the same period, a small yogurt shop in West Hollywood had gone viral. A tiny storefront called Pinkberry launched a tart, sour yogurt that soon acquired a cult following. Lines were forming around the block. It had been started for a small investment only months previously. Pinkberry built a following using the relatively new phenomenon of social media and the internet.

Pinkberry's point of differentiation was that its staff served the customer. Unlike TCBY and Yogurtland, where customers drew their own yogurt out of a machine into a cup and added toppings, Pinkberry sliced fresh fruit. Team members spooned the yogurt into a cup and added the toppings to each customer's specifications, similar to the way Subway builds sandwiches to order behind a glass counter. Mavron executives began keeping an eye on Pinkberry.

I was told by a Mavron board member that Starbucks did not have plans to grow any of their current stable of brands (other than Starbucks) into global retail chains. Potbelly was divested, and eventually, Teavana and La Boulange were closed down altogether while Seattle's Best pivoted into being a supermarket packaged goods brand, rather than a retail play. The point of Mavron since its inception had been to find another category to disrupt at retail in the same way Starbucks did with coffee.

By 2008, piles of cash had been amassed to make a play for Pinkberry, but some Mavron board members wanted to pursue a more upscale, luxury brand better complementing Starbucks as a best-in-class leader. Starbucks admired Godiva's name recognition, coupled with its dual revenue streams from both retail boutiques and wholesale accounts, making Godiva's business model identical to Starbucks'. Both are extremely high-margin businesses with unlimited global growth potential.

By this time, I had gone to work for Leonidas Chocolate. Almost as soon as I started working at the new firm, I received a telephone call from the chairman of Leonidas, asking me to assist the board in acquiring Godiva.

Behind the scenes, I contacted people at Godiva who I had nurtured relationships with. I quickly determined that, much to my surprise, a sale would be considered. A $20 million cash deposit would have to be placed in escrow in order to even examine Godiva's books. Godiva was not going to be wasting time with potential buyers who were not qualified. Proof of funds was required as well; this was to be an all-cash transaction. Under these terms, Godiva could limit the number of exploratory meetings that would be needed to take place with potential purchasers.

With no hesitation, the Leonidas Board agreed to proceed with a $20 million wire transfer. NDA's were signed, and the limited amount of due diligence that would be needed under these extraordinary circumstances began.

In compliance with US laws, Godiva announced they were putting themselves up for sale. Soon Godiva informed Leonidas that another party had met the threshold to enter into talks—without naming who the other party was. That meant Mavron had also wired $20 million into escrow. I think my contact on the Mavron board, knowing I had been running Godiva, wanted me to tell Starbucks how much Godiva was really worth and how much to bid. But I couldn't do that! I was trying to buy Godiva on behalf of the crazy, insanely rich Greek family that owned Leonidas. And if we were successful, it meant that I'd be managing Godiva a second time.

In a surprising twist, Dr. Cherng, founder and, by this time, majority shareholder of Panda Express, offered to write a blank check to buy Godiva based on his confidence in what had been my former business plan that I had reviewed with his representative all those years ago.

Dr. Cherng started a bidding war by making the first opening offer of $400 million. The ground rules set by Godiva were that offers had to be made in $100 million increments. Leonidas was informed the floor was now at $500 million, which we gladly bid because I valued Godiva at about $1 billion, but I wanted a bargain acquisition. Starbucks then offered $600 million, and Panda Express countered with $700 million. We knew that Starbucks must have made a highest-and-best final offer of $800 million, because once Godiva informed us that we would need to offer $900 million cash to remain in the bidding, we knew Panda Express as the previous high bidder wouldn't have further bid against themselves, and there were no other vetted bidders.

Leonidas's board pulled out of negotiations. Our $20 million deposit was refunded. A $500 million investment would have represented taking on a new division valued at half of Leonidas's $1 billion valuation, and that would have been OK. But $900 million was more money than the board wanted to spend at the time. I think history will prove I was right, but the Leonidas family believed in conserving cash, which is why they had plenty of it.

What happened next stunned the industry. At that point, a wild card entry came onto the scene. Yildiz Holdings, a lumber company in Istanbul, offered $1 billion. Published reports confirmed their offer was $800 million in cash plus the assumption of $200 million in debt. Starbucks and Panda Express did not counter. Yildiz acquired Godiva. Sometimes this is typical in big business. Until numbers get to be over $1 billion, conglomerates such as Yildiz feel an acquisition will not be meaningful to the bottom line.

Reflecting back, I think the most interesting thing to wonder about is what Godiva would have been or could have been under Dr. Cherng's ownership. I want readers to fast-forward, reading this chapter in today's context of events, with Yildiz closing all of Godiva's US stores. Will readers feel the same way I do, considering Godiva's legacy to have been squandered?

The postscript for me is the old saying, "There is no such thing as a coincidence." For the past several years, Panda Express corporate has been ordering their Christmas gifts from KC

Chocolatier, the brand I now own. I wonder if Dr. Cherng has been watching us, all along, all these years. It would make sense that if he appreciated fine chocolate then, he appreciates fine chocolate now.

Chapter 15

THE DEVIL SELLS CHOCOLATE

There is a reason why most Leonidas stores are gone from the US. Leonidas's business model did not work. Leonidas sold chocolate through resellers. Resellers were senior Leonidas Chocolate store owners authorized to place their chocolate orders with the factory. Resellers then re-sold chocolate to other junior Leonidas store operators, not authorized to order from the factory, who could only order through their reseller. Resellers earned a contractually stipulated margin of 10 percent on resales. The rationale was that resellers would find additional points of sale, motivated by earning their 10 percent gross margin on an ever-increasing number of distribution points. Most importantly, when working with a new customer, resellers theoretically handled all of the training and did all of the "hand-holding" when new store owners had questions, which was inevitable.

Even a casual reader can see the obvious initial problem with this system. Leonidas stores that were not resellers paid 10 percent more for chocolate. Since all flagship stores were contractually obligated to sell at the same manufacturer's suggested retail price, resellers made 10 percent more gross profit than the shops they provided chocolate to.

In Europe such disparity had not been a problem during Leonidas's formative years. Resellers were the first batch of store owners who "seeded" the brand in various countries by pioneering the first Leonidas shops. Leonidas's corporate salespeople could not be experts on every country in Europe and utilized resellers as its brand ambassadors to uphold policies and maintain consistency. It was up to resellers in the field to identify suitable new store locations to be managed by enthusiastic operators and to reject an applicant that would not be a good fit for the brand.

Resellers took delivery of large chocolate orders by truck. Some of the inventory was meant for the resellers' own Leonidas shops and the extra was back-stock to keep on hand to resell to their other Leonidas sales points in the region. The reseller really did earn their 10 percent margin back in the day because those first-wave shopkeepers took orders, delivered product, and invoiced, taking the risk for payment. Resellers were also liable for damaged goods.

Only resellers could sit on the Dealer Council. Dealer Council was a prestigious body of heavy hitters who owned dozens if not hundreds of Leonidas stores as the years progressed. Dealer Council met once a year with hosting duties rotating through the various countries where resellers operated. The meetings would determine policy affecting all stores on matters ranging from price increases to new product research and development, seasonal window displays, brand extensions such as ice cream, and most importantly, allowing any new resellers into the system. Keep in mind Leonidas paid for all of this and treated the Dealer Council as its de-facto board.

Resellers I was responsible for managing had been with Leonidas since the beginning. In Miami was an individual who had been on the cover of *Time* magazine. He imported caviar, wine, and other luxury goods by arranging his own containers from Europe to Florida. Leonidas was his exclusive chocolate because we specialized in bulk, manufacturing a line of over one hundred chocolates. On a bizarre note, his business was virtually all bulk. Miami customers wanted to receive loose chocolates to put on trays and pass around at banquets as if a chef had made it in-house. When you realize that a container holds 720,000 pieces of bulk, that's a lot of loose chocolate!

A lovely couple in Chicago were from Sweden and France. They used to take me to dinner when I would visit Chicago to see their new stores in Water Tower Place, Wilmette, and Evanston. I kept a wardrobe log to make sure I never repeated an outfit for them because they noticed. The husband is truly, I suspect, the world's first trillionaire, and there really is such a thing even if the public doesn't know what comes next after billionaire. His software company runs the software used by other software companies to create software. The wife loves chocolate and created a dynasty of retail shops with Leonidas being among her stable of prestige brands.

Nobody worked harder than the San Francisco reseller. He would show up at his store at 3:00 a.m. during Christmas, set up knock-down tables throughout the customer areas wherever there was room (because the stock room was overflowing), and prepack enough chocolate boxes to fill his stores' shelves for that day to support customer demand. At 10:00 a.m. when staff arrived, this reseller got in his van and drove around the Bay Area delivering re-orders to his sales points that needed more stock.

This made me begin to realize that US resellers wanting to do tremendous volume were mimicking the trend in Europe and were merely becoming truck drivers. Resellers in Europe would send a truck to Brussels to pick up chocolate orders, then drive back to their country to deliver pre-orders along a route which was by now densely populated with Leonidas locations. France alone had six hundred stores. By the time a truck driver was done with his route, it would be time to drive back to Brussels again to start over.

A reseller's role was designed to function as a highly experienced Leonidas shopkeeper, managing a prototype flagship store that could be used as a training store where new operators could spend a week in training. On paper, resellers were to track sales trends, prepare reports on best-selling chocolates, comparative shop competitors, and come up with new marketing initiatives which could be implemented at the store level. Resellers could also test products before release to the entire network. But in actuality, European resellers had long ago sold their own stores and were merely acting as suppliers, distributing product for a 10 percent margin while no longer putting in the hard work of business development. They were truck drivers.

Long gone were the days of the resellers actually drumming up business because dozens of leads arrived at the factory unsolicited weekly from people wanting to open Leonidas stores. Dealer Council split up the leads among themselves—except for when a request to open in a new territory came along, in which case I and the other country managers handled follow-up. New SAP software I insisted on had been set up by this time, so each store was now placing their orders on-line directly to the factory using a Leonidas intranet portal. Resellers were literally doing nothing that Leonidas couldn't have done had corporate been handling store operations directly.

Therefore, the additional 10 percent margin resellers were earning was causing a great deal of animosity within the Leonidas system. Stores not designated "resellers" were told they could never become resellers for a number of reasons. Those reasons given included high-sales volume targets, mystery shopper scores, and a requirement that being a reseller was a status only designated for multi-unit operators. All of that made sense in a way. There truly were some first-time business people who had no idea how to run a store. Many Leonidas shopkeepers would have run their business into the ground without the support network of being able to reach out to fellow Leonidas store owners and to their reseller.

But the modern view, and the way I looked at it, was that a very small group of store owners were preventing the rest of the Leonidas system from earning a full margin. If resellers made 70 percent, and non-resellers made 60 percent, why should the 10 percent come from the non-resellers? Let the factory rebate 10 percent to the resellers, so all stores could make 70 percent. By 2006, Leonidas had outgrown Godiva. Leonidas corporate could financially afford to take whatever steps were necessary to position the brand for sustainable growth not just in Europe but worldwide. That was what I was brought in to do.

Resellers were not franchisees either. They were licensees who had signed licensing agreements, which did not call for payments of any type of royalties. Resellers were piggybacking off of Leonidas's growth without helping underwrite any of the costs to support that growth. In the US, rest assured that system would have been the other way around had I set it up originally: resellers would have been paying Leonidas something like a 7 percent licensing fee for use of the name plus 3 percent in advertising co-op monthly. I believed resellers should have been paying us.

The breaking point came when it was proven factually that there was no pathway for a non-reseller to be pulled out from under a reseller to become a reseller. No resellers wanted to give up their override on any store they were supplying. I asked for an example of this situation ever occurring, and no one could present even a single instance. To me and to the non-resellers, it was clear that the future of Leonidas was being sacrificed because there was no next generation of leadership being groomed to take over store operations.

Actually, it was entirely possible for a new, first-time store owner to be designated as a reseller from the get-go on day one. They'd simply have to open in a territory that did not have any Leonidas stores. Just as previous generations had to do the hard work of building up a brand, the opportunity was there in South America, Australia, Asia, the Middle East, and the South Pacific. But people wanted to take advantage of the strength of an already strong brand and basically leech off the success that resellers had spent decades building. Nobody wanted to move to Brazil or Mexico to open stores, areas which in my opinion would have done extremely well. The entrepreneurial spirit and drive was missing among people who completely overlooked and undervalued the hard work that it took for resellers to accomplish success.

That is where I came in. The USA was wide open for growth. I picked up the tab out of my North American budget to host Dealer Council two consecutive years in a row, both times in Santa Monica. The first year we bought out The Ambrose Hotel, and the second year we took over the ballrooms and guest rooms at the JW Marriott Le Merigot Santa Monica beach resort. If a tape recording existed of those proceedings, based on the resellers' verbally violent attacks, you'd think I was the devil selling chocolate. I simply explained that we weren't doing things the same way anymore. That's all. It was the dawn of a new age. I pointed out why the European reseller system was not going to work in America.

First of all, Europe is compact. Many European countries are a very short drive to Belgium. But in the US, a reseller in Los Angeles, for example, was not going to have a method to supply a non-reseller in Phoenix. Logistically all orders were shipping directly from the factory in Brussels to each of the US stores rather than shipping to the reseller for distribution. Secondly, I was handling the leads. Thirdly, store operators were entering their own orders into the SAP portal (rather than having their reseller place orders with the factory). US resellers had not been fulfilling the three traditional responsibilities that EU resellers had been handling on behalf of their stores. Carrying out these duties of distribution, prospecting, and writing orders provided the justification for EU resellers to add their 10 percent margin. By comparison, what exactly were US resellers doing to grow a stagnant brand?

I was fine with keeping the existing US resellers at seventy points. They had made half-million-dollar investments into building each of their flagship Leonidas stores. But make no mistake, the only way existing resellers were going to increase their volume was by opening more of their own stores and increasing sales at existing stores. New investors coming into the pipeline would be activated in territories far enough away from existing resellers that everyone would have room to grow for decades with no overlap. I had to approve every location.

This conversation was shorthand for, "every Leonidas customer is going to be a reseller."

The existing group of resellers had fooled Leonidas corporate for a long time into thinking that they were going to build more locations in order to maintain the status quo. One of the first things I did was to visit each store, meet with each reseller, and set down a timetable for when their next store was going to have to open by. No resellers would agree to open any new stores! They all had it in their minds that they were going to wait for "new" operators to join the system, be placed under one of them as a reseller, and make 10 percent without having to invest any further. This had in fact been going on for years and is why there had been zero growth in the US.

Next, I dropped the nuclear bombshell, stating that there were no territory exclusives and no radius restrictions. If an investor presented me with a business plan to open a location in a metropolitan area already served by an existing reseller, then there would be two resellers in a city. We were not—repeat, *not*—going to be blocked from growing store count in world capitals such as Los Angeles, Miami, and New York. I advised resellers who did not want that to happen, to start building stores.

What happened next proves that the cream always rises to the top. Within three years after those two Dealer Council meetings took place, two sisters from Hawaii with a passion for the chocolate café concept, managed to single-handedly find the financing to open ten Leonidas stores throughout metropolitan Los Angeles. Based on such strong performance, there was no need for me to approve bringing in any new investors into the Southern California market.

Where could I find more investors? I had to get creative. The business partners serving on Dealer Council were known elements so I started with them. The gentleman who opened six stores in the Netherlands was going through a divorce. His ex-wife was going to get the stores in the divorce. He wanted to start over in a new country outside the jurisdiction of Dutch courts, so future income would be all his. I suggested Toronto because we had a great location waiting in the central business district. I gambled that nobody would want Toronto besides someone already accustomed to the cold weather. This person took the store sight unseen. My idea worked.

I got a lead on which reseller to approach next once I started asking a lot of questions about the convoluted records on my monthly North American sales reports. The reseller operating multiple New York stores was also the reseller for London. That sounded to me like a well-capitalized partner who had already expanded once.

Gems of ideas come from the most unlikely places and this was one of those times. I had to go to New York for some focus groups and marketing research trials that had been set up by our ad agency. The New York reseller and I met while I was there, and I asked what ideas he had for expansion. He nonchalantly pointed out that there had been no history of wholesale activity in the US the entire time he had been operating the New York store. This reseller wanted to partner on setting up a rate card to begin selling Leonidas to retail chains such as department stores, gourmet markets, and gift shops for a 10 percent markup. Talk about everything coming full circle: now we were back to fulfilling the original mission of why resellers were created, namely for them to drum up new accounts in an entrepreneurial spirit.

The New York operator agreed to bear all the costs of prospecting: sending samples, flying to meetings, and if necessary, leasing a small temperature-controlled warehouse. There were two kinds of reactions from retailers he contacted. In Manhattan, gift basket companies, boutique grocers, and coffee houses ordered because they liked the convenience of having local access to a global brand as an add-on to their other products. However national retail chains based on the East Coast had no interest. That was because of Leonidas's packaging. And I had to agree with them.

While my experiment in New York did not immediately yield its intended consequences regarding sales, all was not lost because it did help me make the case for better packaging for the US. Based on feedback from our New York reseller, I had the ammunition I needed to go back to Brussels and call for a complete overhaul of Leonidas prepackaged gift boxes.

Leonidas met with many packaging consultants who designed chocolate box prototypes that all kept coming out with printing on them. I could not understand why European packaging firms thought it was OK to propose having anything other than the Leonidas logo on the lid of our boxes. I saw phrases like "Fresh Belgian Chocolate," and "100% Pure Cocoa Butter," printed in bas-relief somewhere adjacent to the brand's logo. I was incredulous and got to the bottom of why. Some marketing people in Belgium kept telling the packaging designers to do that as part of the brief. I called the entire marketing team to the Food Show in San Diego and pronounced they were off the project, and I was going to take over and design the boxes in the US myself.

The two primary improvements I made to Leonidas boxes were using a rigid set-up box rather than the old flimsy folding box which looked cheap, and we printed with matte ink instead of glossy ink for a subdued, rich look. With the perfect matching ribbon, voila, we had something to work with that could compete against other chocolate lines in New York such as Maison du Chocolat, Charbonnel et Walker, and MarieBelle.

While waiting for a container of my newly designed empty packaging to be transported by sea from China to Brussels, so we could photograph the U.S. line and create an American Leonidas brochure, I had been renting out my Santa Monica home to a movie studio for a feature film shoot. The studio wanted a long-term lease of several years, so the director could move in because he loved my house so much. I had to decide where I would move if I agreed. I decided to say "yes" to the studio and moved to larger quarters adjacent to Beverly Hills in an area of Los Angeles known as Hancock Park.

My new residence was a replica of a seventeenth century Spanish mission. My property shared a driveway with the house next door. Upon driving up the driveway from the street along the property line, my next-door neighbor could turn right into her garage, and I could turn left into my garage.

My next-door neighbor who shared the driveway was Meghan Markle. At the time, NBC aired its popular game show *Deal or No Deal* at 1:30 p.m. weekday afternoons. Meghan was starring as the spokesmodel on the show.

Meghan was the queen of marketing. She liked to hold fund-raisers for various causes that were important to her. Meghan threw big parties often attended by industry people who could make donations. It didn't hurt to have a beautiful home to entertain in. Her residence was modern Hollywood style.

Sometimes Meghan would order Leonidas Chocolates to set out for guests. Her favorite was our line called Les L's, which the factory tried to say roughly translated from French to Flemish to English as "Angel's Wings." Les L's were bite-sized chocolates molded in the shape of cherub wings with dessert flavors as fillings: crème brûlée, tiramisu, chocolate mousse, and chocolate lava cake. Unfortunately, the public did not like Les L's, and the collection didn't even last one full season, being replaced by Les Coupes. Les Coupes fillings were the same four chocolate flavors, except presented in a miniature chocolate cup. I could never understand why the shape made any difference.

The nearest Leonidas store to the street Meghan and I lived on was in Hollywood on Larchmont Boulevard. Ron Tutor owned Miramax Pictures and knew about the Hollywood store's secret celebrity entrance off the alley (he drove a low-slung Rolls Royce convertible). Mr. Tutor liked to come in and do his shopping without having to mingle with customers. One year he ordered Leonidas by the case to be sent to the Cannes Film Festival. Miramax was sponsoring the American Pavilion, and he planned a champagne and chocolate-tasting party.

Our spokesmodel who appeared on Leonidas posters was invited to Cannes to pass around trays of chocolates during the party. As a surprise we made special "Miramax" logo chocolates, printing the image on top using tinted cocoa butter. They were butterscotch, one of the flavors in the plot of the movie *Chocolat,* which had been a recent Miramax release. The model reported back after the trip saying Mr. Tutor doesn't like chocolate! She couldn't get him to try one. In an interesting twist, our Leonidas spokesmodel's next job was appearing on *Deal or No Deal.*

Chapter 16

THERE'S THE RIGHT WAY, THE WRONG WAY, AND THE LEONIDAS WAY

"If so-and-so said it, it must be true" is my sarcastic catch phrase for instances when people in an organization report to me that "so-and-so" said something to them as if it were the gospel truth when in fact, I know that the statement or opinion being passed on is completely wrong. We may have all known someone who purports to be an authority on a subject and insists that they will give the marching orders. For some reason, when the staff attorneys at Leonidas talked, everyone else listened because they were lawyers. I did not.

Leonidas's motto seemed to be, "sue first and ask questions later." It came as no surprise when Leonidas's lawyer in Belgium gave me a legal project, "recreational litigation." I had to provide ninety-days' notice to resellers in the US stating that their reseller agreements were being terminated and replaced by an updated version. A few resellers were late in signing, and the attorney called me threatening to sue them. I thought to myself, "Where?" I doubted whether a foreign entity could file a complaint in the US courts because of jurisdiction. If Leonidas's lawyer started calling resellers himself, he could have been practicing as a "non-attorney lawyer," the legal term for a person having not passed the US bar exam but representing themselves as an attorney.

Yet legal contracts drafted by counsel had to form the basis for licensing agreements I used in America because there did have to be consistency in Leonidas's global business model. Having never been to law school, I had to find a way to use Belgian documents as source documents for creating US documents, and I became rather adept at it. That experience came to good use when another situation arose regarding a document that had been drafted in Belgium which was intended to be applied in America. The backstory about how that situation came about, began when a new hire started working at Leonidas in Brussels.

It is probably not uncommon for people in the workforce to be able to relate incidents about ambitious professionals they have known who tried to get ahead through unscrupulous methods of backstabbing and disloyalty. My particularly "delicious" example of an incident when this happened to me is about a new hire pretending to be nice to my face while secretly jockeying to create an executive position working alongside me in the USA! This person did not know me well enough to understand that I will always have the last laugh, the final word, and that the only outcomes of any "chocolate wars" are going to be outcomes that are favorable to me.

It all started when I was tipped off by several US Leonidas store owners who phoned me saying that something was going on behind the scenes. My resellers provided dates when they had sent emails to certain departments in Brussels only to have those messages mysteriously forwarded to a new person working in the European division. How odd! Why would anybody at Leonidas's corporate headquarters want to intercept my team's emails? The nonsensical responses coming back directed people who were supposed to email a report to Brussels every other Wednesday to instead fax the report to Los Angeles on alternating Fridays. Fortunately, my US team had been trained well enough on protocols that people knew to disregard such instructions and carried on as usual.

It did not take long to figure out who the mystery figure diverting emails was. The chairman called me to review US sales figures for an upcoming board meeting. He was very happy with our numbers and commented on how poorly European sales were doing in comparison. The chairman said that "a new colleague" had volunteered to fly over to accompany me and observe on a tour of US stores that had long been in the planning stages. The idea was to see firsthand what we were doing to stimulate sales and report back on those promotions to the other country heads.

My long-winded response took about twenty minutes to a half-hour. I explained that the idea did not make any sense because I spent hours—days!—preparing reports for the other country heads in Europe. "Wasn't anybody reading my reports?" I wanted to know. Besides, the US and Europe are completely different markets, and everything about operations on the two continents needed to be tailored to local audiences, down to nitty-gritty decisions about pricing, sizes of packaging, and even the color of our ribbons. "No," I said, "I won't be having anyone from Europe joining me on this trip" because I had growing suspicions of this new person's motives.

With me, "no" means "no," and "no" does not mean "maybe." Just to make sure no one could plan a surprise visit, I reversed the direction of my trip, starting in Montreal and ending in Miami.

Little did I know terror was about to strike in Miami. Leonidas's store was in Aventura Mall on Turnberry Isle. The center is a retail shrine. I had chosen a hotel in Bal Harbor because it was nearby, and that is where I had once lived. I checked in, dropped my luggage in the room, and changed shoes, putting on a pair of black leather Prada driving shoes with bright silver logo buckles. I was not in the room for more than ten minutes before leaving to meet my reseller.

We met at the reseller's warehouse because the majority of his sales were to wholesale accounts. The warehouse was a single-story jumble of everything imaginable that could be saved up over the years just in case someone might ever need it. I remember standing in the room where the staff assembled gift baskets. Wicker baskets were piled high on shelves along with shrink wrap and shredded paper "grass." I felt a prick on the top of my right foot right under the tongue of my shoe. I thought something like a splinter from one of the old baskets had fallen, and instinctively reached down to brush it off my sock. But nothing was there.

Over the next half-hour as I met the sales team, my foot started hurting. We needed to drive from the warehouse to the store, which was about a half-hour away. By the time I arrived in the mall parking lot, I remember limping as I got out of the car. We sat down in some seats at the store and my foot looked swollen. I said, "I think I got bitten by a spider at the warehouse." Aventura Hospital was almost across the street, and I decided to go to the emergency room.

The nurses took one look and said they could see a point of entry where the spider bit me, and the poison venom went in. It looked like a light red round rash that had not been there that morning. The doctors said they needed to hook me up to an IV and introduce a powerful antibiotic because it was unknown what kind of spider bit me. I was given vancomycin which, it turns out, I am allergic to, but I did not know that. My temperature went up to 103 in a matter of minutes, I turned bright red from head to toe, and I was sweating profusely and feeling I was going to pass out. I told the medical team to stop the IV, which they did. I went back to normal fairly quickly.

Due to this reaction, I had to be admitted to the hospital. It would be necessary to find a different antibiotic that could be administered. I wound up staying in Aventura Hospital for two full weeks. I was quite relieved when the treatment eventually worked, and the swelling in my foot did go down. But the doctor in Miami said I could not fly home yet, and my doctor in Los Angeles agreed, explaining that the change in airplane cabin pressure could be quite serious after a swelling infection. I had to go to my hotel and stay in bed for another two weeks to make sure all the swelling went down. I could not walk without a walker or a cane. I ordered a lot of room service, and people I knew in Miami brought meals from my favorite restaurants.

During this time, I informed Leonidas's insurance company that I had suffered an on-the-job injury. The hospital bill presented when I was released was in excess of $110,000, billed to Leonidas's medical plan. Since I had been admitted through emergency, there was no co-pay.

I prepared my expense reports as usual and submitted the hotel bills not only for the lengthy stay in Miami but also for the week prior staying in Montreal, Toronto, New York, and Washington. When a few weeks went by with no reimbursement check, I followed up with accounting in Brussels, who said they had not received my expense reports. That was strange, but papers do get misplaced, so I sent duplicates and was soon reimbursed.

But I began to wonder: Could the envelope that I mailed have been diverted intentionally? Furthermore, I was not pleased to find out that someone from Leonidas had been physically visiting US stores to "check up" on things while I was hospitalized. Her name was Myrtle. The problem was no one had bothered to clear that with me! Whoever this Myrtle person was had not called me to introduce herself.

I decided to take a page out of Myrtle's book and announced that I would be joining *her* at an upcoming Leonidas company retreat in the Black Forest of Germany. Our leadership team stayed at the breathtaking Althoff Grandhotel Schloss in Bensberg outside of Cologne.

At some point Eric, the chairman, ran into me and said he wanted to introduce me to Myrtle. We had drinks in a castle corridor set amongst suits of armor and plaster coats-of-arms décor. What was interesting is that Myrtle was cordial in person. But she made my skin crawl, and my intuition was that she was up to no good. I could tell.

On the last day of the retreat, some members of the board asked me to help them solve a "problem." It seemed that Myrtle's husband was getting transferred to Hartford by the company he worked for. Myrtle wanted to go too but could not because she did not have a visa and without it, she would not be able to work in the US.

My response was decisive and swift. "That's not our problem," I said. "Myrtle's husband will have to decide if he wants to live in Hartford alone. If not, he can decline the transfer." I asked what this had to do with me?

I found it comical that Leonidas was possibly the world's only chocolate company with a fulltime attorney on staff. Why does a chocolate factory need a lawyer? Papers I was soon shown were yet another example of what Leonidas staff in Europe spent their days working on (no wonder sales were bad). I was given a copy of a letter the lawyer had drawn up to "sponsor" Myrtle's transfer from Brussels to Connecticut. The letter was a draft copy addressed to US Immigration and Naturalization, which could only be signed by me as the US CEO. In order to justify her visa application, the two-page document outlined supposed responsibilities Myrtle would carry out in the US that only *she* was capable of performing.

I categorically denied having any part in this fraud being perpetrated. I found strong language to explain that what Leonidas was doing was illegal on many levels. Not only was Myrtle not actually going to be working for Leonidas, Myrtle, in fact, I came to find out, had no skills, no education, and no experience. She did not even know the name of our best-selling chocolate (Manon Café—mocha with a whole crunchy nut)! Suddenly it all made sense. Myrtle had been lobbying for a way to get to move to the US by making it appear that I needed "help" managing the brand. It was entirely probable that she had also been at the very least undermining me and at worst sabotaging my chain of command.

Grabbing the letter, I surprised everyone by saying, "Yes—I'll send a letter to Immigration."

As soon as I got back to Los Angeles, I took the letter that Leonidas's attorney had written, and re-wrote it by adding negatives in front of every legal point that had to be made. I turned the document into an anti-sponsorship document, so I could mail the letter to US Immigration to persuade them to reject rather than approve Myrtle's application. And she would never know why her visa application was turned down had I not written this book.

What I meant in Germany when I said I would send a letter was that I would send a true and correct letter stating actual facts that US authorities needed to be aware of when assessing Myrtle's visa application. Myrtle left the meeting in Germany thinking I was in support of her scheme that violated international border controls. Below are excerpts from my version of the letter, as re-written by me prior to being sent certified mail, return receipt requested:

June 5, 2008
U.S. Department of Homeland Security
US Citizenship and Immigration Services
Vermont Service Center
75 Lower Welden Street
St. Albans, VT 05479

Petitioner: Leonidas Limited
Beneficiary: [redacted]

Dear Officer:

This letter is in denial of support for a Petition for Nonimmigrant Worker (Form I-129) to secure L-1A nonimmigrant classification on behalf of Ms. [redacted], to ensure that she may not enter the country to serve temporarily in the U.S. in the Executive capacity of Director with Leonidas Limited.

THE PETITIONER

Leonidas Limited is a wholly owned (100%) and controlled subsidiary of S.A. Confiserie Leonidas

N.V., the foreign employer. As such, Leonidas Limited intends to circumvent the regulatory definition of a qualifying subsidiary under the Immigration and Nationality Act of 1990 for L-1 intracompany transfers.

THE TEMPORARY U.S. ASSIGNMENT

Leonidas Limited's ("Leonidas") wrongful attempt to employ Ms. [redacted] in the U.S. in the capacity of Director by categorizing her assignment as temporary in the US is fraudulent. Ms. [redacted] presence in the U.S. would take away American jobs from US citizens as part of an illegal structural diversification and expansion into the U.S. market through coordinated efforts with the head office in Belgium.

In this role, Ms. [redacted] does not qualify as a Multinational Executive within the terms of INA §101(a)(15)(L) on the basis of the following:

(A) Ms. [redacted] will in fact not direct the management of the organization or a major component or function of the organization;

Bradford A. Yater (myself) has and will continue to exercise ultimate responsibility for developing Leonidas U.S. sales strategies, policy, and all aspects of business development for the U.S. operation.

Ms. [redacted] proposed position in the U.S. constitutes international visa fraud in that her entire visa application contains material omissions about her intent to overstay her visa.

(B) Ms. [redacted] background is disqualifying

Ms. [redacted] has no unique qualifications or credentials to hold any position in management. To the contrary, she is a new employee working in the European division with no prior experience in the chocolate sector and no familiarity with the US market who does not consider this assignment to be temporary.

MY BACKGROUND AND QUALIFICATIONS

As CEO of Leonidas Limited and Board Member of Leonidas Dealer Council, for both of which I am bonded and insured as the primary point of contact, I make final decisions regarding employment of US personnel. I hold an MBA from Rollins College, and served thirteen years as a US executive at Godiva Chocolatier, a Fortune 500 company publicly traded on the New York Stock Exchange. I was CEO of the NASDAQ-traded publicly held retail chain Kelly's Coffee, holding much of the firm's equity. No individual from another country is more qualified than myself to lead Leonidas Limited, part of a chocolate retail chain operating 1,500 locations in Europe, North America, Asia, the Caribbean, the Middle East, and the South Pacific.

CONCLUSION

It is imperative that appropriate government agencies act swiftly and in coordination to block Ms. [redacted] from arriving in the USA. My recommendation is for [redacted] name to immediately be placed on the "No Fly List." As it is my duty as a citizen of the United States of America to immediately report suspicious activities to the appropriate government agencies, I further seek an expedited review of Ms. [redacted] visa application in order that it be promptly denied. Based on the foregoing, I respectfully request an irrevocable lifetime denial of Ms. [redacted] Petition for Nonimmigrant Worker to permanently ban Ms. [redacted] from seeking L-1A nonimmigrant classification now or at any time in the future.

Should you have any questions or require any further information, please do not hesitate to contact me the undersigned.

Very Truly Yours,

LEONIDAS LIMITED

By: Bradford A. Yater

Bradford A. Yater MBA

CEO, Leonidas North America

I certainly did not share my version of this letter with anyone at Leonidas in Brussels. To the contrary, I was contacted by U.S. Immigration Department officials and filed an affidavit. Based on my affidavit, Myrtle's name was added to the "No Fly List." She was banned from entering the U.S. for ten years, I was told. I was so happy with the government for listening to a citizen.

Soon after this happened, within a month or two, my reseller in New York forwarded me screen shots of a house for sale in Hartford. The reseller said Myrtle and her husband had bought a house in anticipation of their relocation. "For some reason," they were not able to move after all, and the house was being sold. The address matched the address provided on the original version of the letter prepared by Leonidas's attorney, so I knew that was indeed the house they planned to move into. How presumptuous, I thought, to assume that their plan was going to succeed and that I was going to cooperate.

This situation could have possibly been avoided had people been straightforward in their dealings. It all boils down to people underestimating me and not realizing that I have eyes in the back of my head and *will* find out everything that goes on in my stores, one way or another, sooner or later. Management is not glamourous; management is the daily routine of doing the job to stay on top of running the business. This incident really made me think about whether Leonidas was going to be the best fit for me in the long term because I did not like the way things had been handled.

Even worse than the visa incident, it was unforgiveable to me that no one from Leonidas headquarters ever contacted me during the month I was in Miami to ask how I was doing. The reseller from Aventura Mall did send me a box of Leonidas Chocolate to make me feel better (knowing me well enough to pack it with all dark and all creams—my favorite) and visited me at the hospital. Thinking back, I wonder if that was because he was afraid of being sued by Leonidas to recover the $110,000 in medical bills?

Chapter 17

LEONIDAS BECOMES THE GODIVA OF EUROPE

The world has Leonidas's financially strong store performance to thank for the creation and existence of a retail "secondary market." The phrase refers to the practice of investors buying existing chocolate stores—and the licenses to operate them—rather than going through the construction process of building new stores (and qualifying for a license directly from the licensor—Leonidas, the manufacturer). Prior to Leonidas's introduction of its chocolate café shop format in the US and worldwide, there had not been much of an active market either for entrepreneurs to acquire chocolate businesses or for individual store owners to sell their chocolate businesses. What changed was the profitability of Leonidas's stores as a system, enabling shopkeepers to sell rather than to simply close when it came time to retire. Active investors in the chocolate space began speculating by building stores for the purpose of selling them on the secondary market rather than being operators. Leonidas stores became currency.

My specialty has been helping both buyers and sellers of retail stores determine fair market value in order for a sale transaction of a business to occur. While managing Leonidas, it helped that I was the licensor and got to know the personalities of the sellers, understanding their strengths and what factors motivated them to get into retailing. Promoting Kelly's Coffee provided exhaustive experience working with high-net-worth individuals to structure transactions to acquire stores. From a commercial standpoint I understood what both parties looked for to do a deal.

Sellers almost always have an expectation for how much their business is worth. Advisors such as CPAs use various formulas to arrive at a determination of what they recommend to their clients that the selling price should be. Buyers, on the other hand, compare the cost of buying an existing business against the amount of money it would take to start a comparable business. The difference between these two numbers is where room for negotiation comes into play.

In retailing, the term EBITDA refers to "earnings before interest, taxes, depreciation, and amortization." EBITDA is a bookkeeping term referencing a business's P and L (profit and loss) statement. EBITDA appears on the P and L as an actual line-item on the books. Business owners use accounting software to record monthly revenues and expenses, and the program calculates EBITDA. In theory, the higher the EBITDA, the more profitable the business.

In practice, buyers analyze financial records to determine whether they will be managing the business the way the seller did, because if not, net profit could change. If the seller manages the store on a daily basis but does not pay themselves a salary, only withdrawing loans or disbursing dividends at the end of the accounting year, but a buyer intends to manage the store and put themselves on payroll, EBITDA will be lowered, all other factors remaining equal.

Therefore, I counsel that it is naïve to listen to third-party advisors making general statements to parties in a business sale transaction in which they reinforce a general belief that retail stores trade for two to three times EBITDA. That multiplier could be considered a general guideline but only for purposes of entering into talks. Everyone selling or buying a business must be prepared to understand that ultimately, market forces will set the price at which the business will sell for. When a seller's price is unrealistically high, there will be no buyer—yet.

In other words, once a seller shares the retail financial statements with a prospective buyer, a true dialogue begins between both parties. Numbers do not mean anything without a context to place them in. The numbers provide a "picture" of a business's financial health, and numbers do not lie. But good, bad, or middling, what does the picture reveal about the reasons why an owner may want to sell? And what reasons could a seller provide to help a buyer understand why they would want to purchase a particular business?

One universal truth needs to be understood by *sellers*: a business owner who has taken their money out throughout all of the years they have owned their business shows a less compelling set of books when selling. This type of seller will extract less for their business. When examining the books, look for the types of expenses being charged against the company. I have seen it all—leased cars, college educations, reimbursement of personal credit card balances, and other expenses that had nothing to do with store operations. To be quite frank, businesses operated this way were designed by the owners to show as little profit as possible each year as a way of reducing tax liability. That's fine, but then EBIDTA is minimal, and two to three times nothing is not so much when it comes time to sell.

The universal truth *buyers* need to understand has to do with the seller's entrepreneurial skills being valued and recognized in the abstract as part of a business' worth. Someone wanting to buy a successful store because it is doing well must recognize they will be paying a premium because the seller set the store up for success. The seller found a great location, worked hard for years, and developed a clientele. Part of what the buyer is buying is the intangible "goodwill." As esoteric as that sounds when trying to value a store, clientele is not invisible; it does show up on the books as top-line gross sales. A busy store with many customers, has higher sales figures.

Successful buyers who are able to scoop up trophy businesses are forward thinkers. They do not think like accountants and stare at the books. Entrepreneurs wanting to own their own business develop a business plan outlining ways to increase sales even more. I advise people, "Don't look at the past; we know where this business was. Think about the future. Where can you take this business?"

Highly desirable chocolate cafés and coffee shops often approach one million dollars in annual sales. At an industry average 20 percent net profit if well run, such a store is netting $200,000. From an owner's perspective, that store might be listed for sale at $400,000 to $600,000, which is two to three times net earnings. Factors affecting that range are predominantly the remaining lease term, competitive positioning, and whether or not the seller expects all cash or is willing to carry some financing.

From a buyer's perspective, a start-up chocolate café or coffee shop may be built for $300,000 to $500,000. But how many years will it take for a new location to ramp up sales to $1 million? Is the buyer taking into account that it will take an absolute minimum of one year to find a location, hire an architect, obtain permits, and build the store? That is one year of "no sales." More importantly, is a comparable location available to build a new store in the type of established neighborhood where an existing business is available for sale?

Buyers soon realize that sellers are in a strong negotiating position. Sellers of successful stores do not need to sell. They can continue to operate their highly profitable location, meaning any potential buyer who decides to go into business by starting their own store nearby will have to compete against the seller's store. "Buying out a competitor" is a common reason for buyers to decide to pay a premium to acquire an existing business.

Leonidas contracts gave me final approval over transferring Leonidas licenses. I once spoke with a buyer prior to opening escrow on a fantastic opportunity. The buyer hesitated to invest $200,000 due to the uncertainty over how much money could be earned as a first-time business owner. I realized what the buyer was doing was comparing owning a business with getting a job. This person wanted a paycheck every two weeks, which is the exact opposite of being entrepreneurial. I told the person they'd be better off getting a job because having that type of mentality will not be effective at managing a retail store. They had not thought about what their day-to-day responsibilities would be, mistakenly thinking stores run themselves.

It might appear that the sellers would have been mad at me for finding out they had "no deal." That was rarely the case. Sellers look at their stores as their "baby" that has been nurtured and grown for years, even decades. When entertaining multiple offers, sellers want their stores to wind up in the hands of someone who will carry on their legacy. My best advice to buyers is to portray yourselves as being willing to retain the best of the old while embracing all that is new to take the store to the next level.

Once a seller and a buyer have "found" each other and there is mutual intent to get a deal done, financial terms are often negotiable. Buyers willing to pay the seller's full asking price, could write the offer as being contingent upon some seller financing. 75 to 80 percent of the purchase price might be paid in cash with the remainder paid out over the next two to five years as a percentage of the store's profit. Or, the buyer may pay the seller a consulting fee of $20,000 to $30,000 per year for the next one to two years to advise on business operations.

Mall leases contain a "cure of default" clause which could come in handy in a situation when a seller agrees to participate with some financing, but an inexperienced buyer is too hands-off and does not manage the business profitably. In that case, the seller notifies the landlord that they are defaulting the buyer, curing the default by paying any unpaid back rent, and taking back the business due to non-payment of the note.

I had that situation happen in a mall when the landlord tried to say that because the person who purchased a Leonidas store had not paid rent in three months, the landlord was going to lease the store to someone else. I stated that per the terms of the lease, no, that was not going to happen. The original seller, Dottie, paid the three months' back rent owed and took over the store again (curing the default), managed it for a few months to build up the business, and sold the store a second time! Dottie received $400,000 of the

$500,000 sale price from the first sale transaction because she had carried $100,000 in seller financing. Then Dottie netted another $500,000 the second time she sold the store for all cash! Dottie's pre-tax gain on $900,000 was off-set by capital improvements that had been made over the years, and by the impact of depreciation on FF and E (furnishings, fixtures, and equipment), to potentially reduce tax liability. Further I reminded Dottie to write-off her $100,000 non-collectible debt as a tax deduction. In Dottie's case, selling her Leonidas store may have been more profitable than holding on to it.

I have this advice for buyers who cannot afford to buy an established business, which is always going to cost more than starting a business. Look for a location that was previously rented by a food use of any type, a so-called "second generation" location. That will enable the new business owner to take advantage of the build-out left behind by the previous tenant. Perhaps $100,000 in savings could be realized by not having to pay for installation of costly fire safety systems, electrical panels, plumbing, mechanical systems (air conditioning and heat), a gate, FRP surfaces (required by the health department on walls), sinks, tile flooring, restrooms, and possibly some lighting, doors, stockrooms, and even countertops and cabinets. There have been two cases when Leonidas licensees only had to paint, change out exterior illuminated signage, and install a new menu board to open. All their equipment was leased including a POS system and a credit card machine.

Licensees whose business model is to build stores intending to sell them for a profit do so with the knowledge that there is a pool of buyers who cannot envision where to begin the process of building a store. Such buyers are really looking for established cash flow to carry them through the first year while they learn about the chocolate and coffee business.

Since every business valuation reflects a unique store, no two people will ever come up with the same valuation. Deciding how much a business is worth is not about coming up with the "right" amount; it is about two parties agreeing to come to terms. Ultimately, whether that will happen depends on how much the buyer wants the acquisition. Sellers should not have their feelings hurt when an offer comes in lower than asking price; I urge sellers to think about what that says about their asking price—are their expectations realistic based on the market?

The subject of licensing versus franchising confuses people, but it shouldn't. Licensing is similar to franchising but without any on-going fees in the case of Leonidas. Licensing offers much more freedom to shopkeepers when it comes to adding menu items. Both are extremely valuable systems in the eyes of landlords because the shop owner is not trying to figure things out on their own; each location is based on a proven system of operations, so the landlord knows what to expect. In my experience, licensed and franchised concepts sell at a premium over "mom and pop" stores, which I tell buyers is because so much of the set-up work has already been done for them (establishing a vendor structure, providing recipes, suggesting menu prices).

In the US, the most a Leonidas Chocolate Café has ever sold for was about $700,000. The least a Leonidas Chocolate Café has ever sold for was about $200,000. Believe it or not, both sets of books showed about the same amount of net profit. But, the store that sold for more showed dramatically increasing sales over the last three years prior to the sale while the store that sold for less was losing customers rapidly due to a competitor opening nearby.

In addition, the owner of the higher-valued store had just renewed his lease, but the lower-valued store only had one year left on their lease. Here is the hard fact shopkeepers need to understand: if you don't have a lease, you don't have anything to sell. Licensed and franchised retail stores are tenants on leases; they do not own the real estate. Licensed and franchised retail store owners do not own the concept; the corporate brand owns the concept. The advice I give sellers is to renew their lease for as long a term as possible and *then* sell. It sounds counterintuitive but is a critical step.

Renewing a favorable lease is the surest way sellers command top dollar. Which means that when buyers realize a seller did not renew their lease, the buyer should meet with the landlord to make sure they will be able to sign a lease at terms similar to the current lease when the current lease ends. When bank financing is being used for part of the purchase price, any bank will expect to see either an LOI (Letter of Intent) or a lease, confirming occupancy costs as presented in your business plan.

SBA (Small Business Administration) financing remains an excellent source of funds to buy a business. I have assisted in preparing packets for submission to the SBA on over twenty-five deals. SBA loans are government-guaranteed; therefore, banks have no reason *not* to make the loan. 20 percent of the purchase price in cash is required as a down payment. Knowing this, a straightforward calculation may be made as to how much a buyer might spend on purchasing a business, knowing how much cash is available to put down. Credit worthiness is the other primary factor taken into consideration, but only to the extent that credit scores affect the interest rate, meaning a low credit score will not necessarily block a loan from being made.

I suggest phoning several local banks to ask if they are what is known as a "direct" SBA lender. There are two types of lenders participating in the SBA program: direct and indirect. A direct lender is a high-volume SBA lender who is pre-authorized by the SBA to approve loans at the local level. Indirect lenders, on the other hand, must submit SBA loan packages to Washington for approval. Both require exactly the same amount of paperwork. The difference is speed. A direct lender approves a loan in as little as two months. An indirect lender can take up to six months. A seller will have to agree to keep their business off the market for the duration while a buyer is waiting for SBA funding. With a non-refundable deposit, most reasonable sellers will understand why a buyer needs a two-month window of exclusivity to tender the balance in full.

My recommendation for buyers is to seek a business that is part of a licensed or franchised system because major national brands are pre-approved by the SBA. The SBA only needs to evaluate the borrower—not the borrower *and* the business—in these situations. SBA fast-tracking for "name brands" is part of the SBA's mission to help grow the US economy since retailing constitutes 66 percent of America's GNP. The Kelly's Coffee brand was pre-approved by the SBA.

Owning your own business can be a dream come true for many people. For those who say one store cannot generate enough income, I advise them to plan on becoming a multi-unit operator. Another option is to find an emerging concept offering territory rights, enabling the licensee to sell sub-licenses within a geographic region. With encouragement from reading this book, the truly ambitious entrepreneur might decide to create a concept as I did and become the licensor.

Chapter 18

I WROTE THE BOOK ON CHOCOLATE

My contract with Leonidas was coming up in a year, and a renewal was not going to happen. I wanted a lot more money. The consensus at Leonidas in general was that people felt like there was really no need for any modernization, that everything was fine just the way it was, and that all the changes I was making were creating more work for people. I had *never* gotten that impression from anyone at Godiva.

I felt the time had come for me to be an owner and not an executive managing someone else's asset. My goal had long been to own a prestige chocolate brand. I decided on a start-up. I was excited to create from scratch what would become my family-owned business' new brand of gourmet Belgian chocolate.

As the undisputed thought leader in the chocolate industry, my profound vision for founding my own chocolate brand was to make chocolate a staple. By the time I was done, every home would have chocolate in the pantry or in the cupboard. I needed every consumer in the world to have chocolate on their shopping list when going to the grocery store. Chocolate would become a necessity like milk, bread, and eggs. I was going to drive demand to make chocolate a part of peoples' daily lives. I was going to make sure chocolate was accessible in every corner of the globe.

Starting KC Chocolatier was my "third act." My inspiration was Colonel Sanders, who popularized fried chicken when he was sixty-five years old and could not afford to retire. His company KFC (Kentucky Fried Chicken) opened 3,000 stores by the time the Colonel died thirty years later—all done at an age when many people are retired. Whenever the final chapter of the KC Chocolatier story is written, some people may see me as a visionary businessperson akin to Colonel Sanders. Skeptics may accuse me of employing fancy marketing to make a nickel's worth of ingredients into a product consistently selling for ninety dollars per pound. But either way, as more-or-less a legend in the chocolate industry, I felt there is always a way to start a chocolate brand no matter how crowded the playing field seems from the outside looking in.

My business plan, based on a lifetime of experience, was to first generate profits by *wholesaling* private label brands to retailers (business-to-business sales). Those profits would be invested into marketing a newly created *retail* brand, "KC Chocolatier" (business-to-consumer sales). None of the firms I had previously managed—Bloomingdale's, Godiva, Kelly's Coffee, Leonidas—incorporated a private-label component into their business model. I was taking a calculated risk based on where an opening was to compete in the market at the time in 2009.

The key to exponential increases in profits in business is knowing how to scale. I was not going to take one step forward and two steps back like Godiva did when they closed all US Godiva stores. First, I sourced a new factory with virtually unlimited production capacity to produce my chocolates in Belgium. Second, I set up an ISO—independent sales office—in Los Angeles. Effective selling required a professional sales organization in the field able to keep up with the factory's ability to produce fine chocolates. ISOs could be replicated on every continent by partners with local expertise. Responsibilities were clearly split. The factory would make chocolate, and I would market chocolate.

Brands begin with a name. Bilateral treaties are in place with many countries so that once a trademark application is approved in one nation, trademark rights are recognized worldwide. The main reason there are so many mediocre names for companies and products, especially cars that sound like alphabet soup, is because choosing a name that is available to trademark has become increasingly difficult. I wanted to choose a name paying homage to the legacy of Kelly's Coffee and Godiva, representing good luck for me. I took the initials "K" and "C" from Kelly's Coffee and added the word "Chocolatier" from Godiva Chocolatier, all done in Godiva gold.

At Godiva, the company's name had been chosen for a number of reasons. It was easy to pronounce in many languages and was available to trademark. Lady Godiva had been a historical figure, so there was an ability to create an iconic logo of the woman with long flowing hair. Similarly, King Leonidas was a Spartan, so the Leonidas logo in the shape of a shield played off of that heritage. But a Greek king is no better than an English lady as a legendary figure to name a Belgian chocolate company after. My goal with the name KC Chocolatier was to emphasize our tagline, "Belgian Chocolate," as much as possible.

People might have said I was crazy for building a company that would be in direct competition with the brand I helped create. But my experience at Godiva also showed me its weaknesses, which allowed me to help KC Chocolatier thrive—while Godiva was barely surviving. KC Chocolatier was willing to produce chocolates for sale under various retailers' brand names, to help retailers build *their* brand awareness. Godiva would never do that because Godiva was marketing the Godiva brand, not other retailer's brands. I am often asked, "Why hadn't anyone else thought of that?"

My marketing efforts helped build our business from a standstill on day one, which I had the courage to attempt, and it also opened the door for a lot of other chocolate companies to launch. "A rising tide lifts all boats" is a saying that comes to mind. There was room for many new chocolate companies as proven by the expanding size of chocolate aisles in modern supermarkets. Why are there so many chocolate brands? Because we all make money!

The chocolate industry's combined advertising campaigns increased awareness enough to achieve a record $18 billion in chocolate sales in 2019 in the US, according to Euromonitor, a leading retail research firm. (2019 was the last year prior to the pandemic for which statistics were available at the time of this writing.) How in the world did such a pure and simple pleasure become such an economic engine? Because every person who has ever shopped at a mall, given a gift, received a gift, or eaten a chocolate has enjoyed one kind of chocolate or another, helping brands achieve dominance and savor the sweetness of success.

According to MarketWatch, Americans cannot get enough of all things chocolate. The trade group estimates Americans buy seventy-five dollars' worth of chocolate and chocolate-related products per person per year. The National Retail Federation assesses that malls with a chocolate retail store are in the top 20 percent of performers among all shopping centers. The Uniform Code Council, a trade group in Washington DC that issues UPC bar codes, reports that 80 percent of market baskets check out with some chocolate in the cart. The war has been won—chocolate is now perceived as a normal part of the American diet, not just a "treat."

In Europe, per capita consumption has grown to double that of the US, reaching eleven pounds of chocolate per person per year. European sales of chocolate were estimated at $35 billion per year in 2021 with the highest percentage of sales coming from elegant European-style molded chocolates, which are projected to be the fastest growing category for European sales of chocolate through 2024, according to projections from ResearchAndMarkets.com, a chocolate retail industry analysis firm.

During the preparation of this manuscript, in January of 2021, Godiva did in fact announce the closure of all of its US stores. My belief that Godiva could not continue operating much further into the future in its current incarnation proved true. I will analyze this as a business decision by giving my spin on what I believe motivated the business' owners in Istanbul to take action.

Godiva's new owners appeared to want to turn Godiva into a mass-market brand. Yildiz management might have felt that Godiva was a household name, so why not capitalize by trading on that familiarity on a daily basis? Yet that strategy diminished the brand because a luxury brand cannot have it both ways: once Godiva Valentine's hearts were available in drugstores for $9.99, fewer shoppers were willing to make a special trip to a fashion mall to pay seventy-five dollars for a Godiva heart. The difference in packaging (velvet versus cardboard) may have been enough to justify the difference in price, but, upon closer scrutiny, the chocolate was different, too. Godiva had started selling two levels of chocolate: "good" pieces in the lower-priced hearts in this example and "better" pieces in the hearts purchased at a mall. That loss of consistency can be confusing for customers.

I believe there should be different brand names when targeting different audiences as in the example above. This explains why I was very careful to keep separate my two-pronged approach: *selling* private-label chocolate to retailers needing to hit a competitive price point, while *marketing* my high-end brand, KC Chocolatier, for gourmet aficionados. Whichever retailers I "sold" private-label chocolate to had to do their own "marketing."

In order for this strategy to work, I needed to take the unusual and expensive step of having both dual air and sea logistics in place as supply chains to distribute to wholesale and retail clients worldwide, large and small. This system enabled KC Chocolatier to produce private label brands for Nordstrom, Williams-Sonoma, Gelson's Supermarkets, and many other major retailers.

KC Chocolatier and the private-label brands KC Chocolatier produces are carefully packaged and priced to mimic lifestyle brand attributes I perfected at Godiva. Godiva customers were telling us how our chocolate made them *feel*. The "secret sauce" at KC Chocolatier is structuring the company's product line as viewed through the lens of its customers. Glittered vintage images on our boxes cause people to reminisce about nostalgic feelings. Thus our "look" positions KC Chocolatier to achieve an emotional reaction from shoppers, making customers *want* to buy our chocolate. Thus, my products bring my career full circle again, satisfying a "want" rather than a "need," a technique I perfected at Godiva.

Once packaging was in place, it was time to create the chocolate! What was KC Chocolatier going to be? I wanted KC Chocolatier to be known as "the people's chocolate," an unintimidating and approachable brand. That meant taking recognizable flavors and presenting them beautifully. From a production standpoint, each chocolate had to be made in two or three steps. Above all, chocolate companies make money by selling certainty; people must be certain they will like at least some of the chocolates in our box, specifically coffee, caramel, nuts, buttercream, and mint. KC Chocolatier's selections are Americanized versions of European traditional best-sellers.

My favorite KC Chocolatier piece is Vienna, vanilla buttercream piped out of a pastry tube between two discs of 77 percent extra dark chocolate with a garnish of roasted cocoa nibs for crunch. Vienna looks like a little ice cream sandwich. Our pieces are so-called "two bite" chocolates, weighing fifteen grams each. This generous piece with eye appeal was romanced by naming it after a popular European capital.

But the best seller turned out to be Axelle, our dark salt caramel. Axelle is a molded piece. From the enrobing line, Bellissimo is a mocha hazelnut cream with a whole hazelnut. A foil wrapping machine enabled KC Chocolatier to create Francesca, a cherry cordial fondant. We needed hand-rolled truffles and started with a 64 percent Peru single-origin dark chocolate truffle, plain with no garnish. The *pièce de résistance* is a line of fresh creams, which have a short shelf life and are rarely available outside of Belgium. Fresh creams have a light, whipped, airy center. Coccinelle is a milk chocolate fresh cream with bits of toffee crunch.

What KC Chocolatier is not is a *nouveau* artisan house. My customers are not guinea pigs to test ideas on. People want their money's worth. This means customers expect all the chocolates in a box to be scrumptious. That is why we will not produce flavors like spicy chili pepper or olive oil with breadcrumbs, just to mention two flavors made by competitors. People may buy experimental types of chocolates once to try them, but they will always come back to their favorite traditional flavors.

Chapter 19

IT CAME FROM THE LAB

Now that I was starting my own chocolate company, and I had linked up with a prominent master chocolatier, it was important for me to understand more about how chocolate was made. I always had been—and would continue to be—a marketer focused on finance, merchandising, logistics, and the interplay between those fields of expertise. KC Chocolatier was going to be more interesting because I had never pro-actively suggested the types of chocolate to make at Godiva or Leonidas. My involvement had been to manage by monitoring and assessing sales trends. Godiva and Leonidas were at least sixty years old, but KC Chocolatier would be all-new.

Growing Cocoa

Theobroma cacao is the cocoa tree originating in the Amazon region. In the seventeenth and eighteenth centuries, cultivation of the cocoa tree spread to the Philippines and the West Indies, and from the nineteenth century cocoa was also cultivated in West Africa, Central and South America, and Asia. The cocoa regions are equatorial since the cocoa tree likes high temperatures and high humidity.

The most important varieties currently cultivated are the criollo and the forastero. The criollo produces the highest-quality bean, which is used in the finest chocolates. The forastero is less susceptible to disease and is by far the most widely cultivated. It produces what is considered industrial or ordinary cocoa.

The cocoa tree is a tall slim tree that can grow to twenty meters. On the plantations, trees are kept pruned to between four and ten meters. The tree bears leaves all year, varying from pale green to deep purple, of varying age and with a life of about one year.

The flowers appear about three to four years after planting on the mature wood of the trunk and branches; they're grouped into so-called fruit cushions. The fertilized flower forms a young fruit that on ripening (five to six months) develops into a yellow, red, or orange pod, depending on the plant variety. Because the tree blooms all year, there are always fruits at every stage of development, from fruit germ to the fully grown ripe fruit. The pods are fifteen to thirty centimeters long and contain thirty to forty cocoa beans, each about two centimeters long.

The mature pod has to be picked by cutting the flower stalk with a sharp knife without damaging the fruit cushions. Pods picked too early produce lower grade cocoa; over-ripe pods are open to disease and unsuitable for the production of commercial cocoa. After picking, the beans ripen for a further week and are only then opened. The flesh between the rows of beans is stripped off and discarded with the pods. Exposure to air causes the cream-colored beans to turn purple, and they are now ready for the fermentation process.

The purpose of fermentation is to ferment the flesh around the beans and allow the precursors of the typical taste and smell compounds to develop. The cocoa beans are piled into huge heaps on banana leaves or in chests and then covered with banana leaves. Wild yeasts and bacteria penetrate the beans and convert the sugar that is still in the pulp surrounding each bean into carbon dioxide and alcohol and eventually into acetic acid. During this process, the cocoa seeds die, losing all power to germinate. At the same time, the original bitter, sharp taste becomes milder, and the color of the bean changes from purple to chocolate brown. The whole process of fermentation and drying takes about six to ten days.

After they have been dried, the beans are packed into jute sacks of sixty to seventy kilograms. The sacks are marked and numbered. A number of samples are taken to assess the quality. Then the cocoa beans are ready for trading on the international market.

Processing from bean to cocoa mass

Before the beans can be processed, they must be perfectly clean. Beans are sieved and dusted. After the cleaning comes the most important phase for the chocolate: the roasting. During the roasting in rotating ovens at one hundred to one hundred fifty degrees Celsius, the cocoa bean develops its characteristic aroma, and some of the acetic acid produced during fermentation evaporates. While still hot, the beans, which have shrunk through moisture evaporation, can now be shelled. A side effect of the roasting process is that the beans are sterilized, and all bacteria and molds are killed.

The hulled kernel or nib of the beans is separated from the shell and passes through a mill. Grinding produces the chocolate liquor. This liquor is stored in tanks. When this chocolate liquor is subjected to high pressure, it separates into cocoa powder and cocoa butter. Despite the name, chocolate liquor has nothing to do with alcohol. It is a dark paste used as a base for chocolate making. The darker the chocolate, the higher the percentage of chocolate liquor.

The production of chocolate

The first stage in the commercial production process for chocolate is making the mash. The mash is a mixture of the various ingredients, which is then kneaded into a smooth dough. Mixing and kneading chocolate liquor, cocoa butter, and sugar produces the basis for plain chocolate: the more bitter the taste, the higher the chocolate liquor content. Milk powder is added to produce milk chocolate. White chocolate contains only cocoa butter, sugar, and milk powder.

After the kneading, the chocolate particles have to be reduced in size, so that the consumer does not experience the chocolate as tasting "gritty." To achieve this, the mash is passed through steel rollers that rotate at ever-increasing speed. This process is responsible for creating the fineness of the finished chocolate, which to a major degree determines its quality.

To further develop the chocolate flavor, crushing is followed by conching. This process was invented in 1890 by the Swiss Rodolphe Lindt. The chocolate mass is kneaded again for several hours, this time coupled with great friction, heat, and aeration. This releases acidity and bitterness, leaving just the true chocolate aromas. The conching stage concludes with the addition of lecithin and cocoa butter. The homogeneous mass produced is liquid at a temperature of thirty-five to forty degrees Celsius. Part of our secret process is knowing how to make the chocolate couverture fluid enough to flow through the factory. It takes just the right combination of lecithin, chocolate mass, and cocoa butter.

Processing of chocolate

KC Chocolatier is not involved in chocolate production per se but has joint ventures with specialist companies to produce chocolate to its recipes, thus ensuring the characteristic taste of KC Chocolatier.

KC Chocolatier receives the chocolate in liquid form and stores it in huge tanks. The fillings for both the bars and the chocolates are prepared in-house. The ingredients are based amongst other things on the old family recipes of our chocolatier, developed in their time by his father and grandfather, so we can look back on more than one hundred years of chocolate-making expertise.

The most common fillings are described below:

Marzipan:	molten sugar mixed with finely ground almonds, often with some pistachio nuts as well
Praliné:	caramelized, finely ground almonds and/or hazelnuts, mixed with milk chocolate
Gianduja:	mixture of very finely ground hazelnuts, almonds, or walnuts, sugar and milk or dark chocolate
Truffle:	mixture of chocolate, cocoa butter, sugar, and cream
Fondant:	mixture of various sugars, water, and confectioner's glucose

Croquant:	caramelized sugar with chopped roasted hazelnuts and/or almonds
Caramel:	caramelized sugar mixed with fresh cream and butter
Fresh Cream:	whipped fresh cream with added butter and glucose
Ganache:	mixture of chocolate and cream, usually with butter
Nougat:	mixture of whisked egg-white, boiled sugar or honey, nuts, and candied fruit

These are the basic fillings for the chocolates. These fillings may be further supplemented with other ingredients such as flavorings, all kinds of fruit, nuts, coffee, and tea. KC Chocolatier's ingredients are wholly natural—no preservatives or genetically manipulated products are added.

To produce the chocolates, the hot chocolate from the tanks first has to be pre-crystallized. It cannot be used immediately because it will harden only very slowly on cooling. First, the chocolate is melted to a temperature of fifty degrees Celsius until the crystal structure of the cocoa butter is totally disintegrated. Then it is cooled to about twenty-eight degrees, thereby strengthening its molecular structure ("tempering"). Finally, the temperature is increased a little so that the crystals form perfect chains. The precise temperature depends on the type of chocolate, but the aim is for the prepared chocolate to have a beautiful rounded taste, that it is easy to work, has a fine sheen, and stores well.

After the tempering, the chocolate can be processed further. KC Chocolatier utilizes two techniques to produce the final chocolates: molding and enrobing.

In molding, a mold is filled with tempered chocolate. Then the mold runs over vibrating tables to remove any air bubbles and then passes through a cooling tunnel. Once out of the tunnel, the mold is inverted, and the excess chocolate shaken out until the casing walls are the correct thickness. The casings are then cooled in a cooling tunnel to a temperature of about ten degrees Celsius. When the correct degree of cooling has been achieved, the filling is dispensed into the casing by machine. Shaking distributes the filling evenly. A chocolate sealing layer is then applied, and it is passed through the cooling tunnel for a final time. After some fifteen minutes, the finished chocolates can be removed from the mold. The same procedure is used for filled bars.

In enrobing, things are done the other way round. First, a base is made onto which a filling is laid. The base passes through a cooling tunnel. After that it passes through a bath of tempered chocolate. Then a vibrator ensures that the chocolate coating is the right thickness and evenly distributed. The decoration is usually applied by hand, and finally the chocolates go through the cooling tunnel.

We have six production lines: three molding lines, two enrobing lines, and one flow-packing line to package chocolates individually. Eighteen tons of chocolate are produced per day (three shifts), or seventy tons of chocolate bars are produced per day (three shifts).

The chocolates and bars are ready to be packed and shipped following a final, thorough quality control. Finished chocolates gently drop onto a rubber-lined conveyor belt equipped with bumpers resembling a pachinko game. These bumpers gently line up the pieces single file on the belt, so they may drop precisely into plastic trays lining cardboard boxes. Finished chocolates weigh fifteen grams on average. Thirty pieces should equal a pound.

Refrigerated trucks transport chocolates from Brussels to Paris airport. Air France flies monthly deliveries to the US. This system was set up identically at both Godiva and Leonidas.

Much of KC Chocolatier's cocoa originates in Tanzania. A trade secret is not the ingredients but the order in which ingredients are mixed. Our technique extends the freshness of chocolates without the added use of stabilizers, preservatives, or any type of artificial ingredients.

The 12,000 square meter (130,000 square foot) factory producing our chocolate was newly built in 2008. Its design was based upon principles of sustainability, which are one of the brand's core values. Water runoff from production is filtered through bamboo in the ground surrounding the factory, a bio-fermentation system enabling cleaned water to be channeled out to neighboring farmlands. All energy used is renewable, with about 30 percent of the plant's energy coming from 2,987 solar panels mounted on the roof. At the parking lot entrance is an electronic meter displaying the number of CO_2 emissions saved to date by choosing renewable energy (currently 1,309 tons per year saved in CO_2 emissions). One hundred and fifty employees work full-time at the plant making chocolate.

The modern factory is one of the most accredited chocolate production facilities in Belgium, winning the Laurel Award for "most energy conscious" design in Flanders, the region where Brussels is located. Certifications include Beyond Chocolate (sustainability initiative), ISO 14001 (environmental management), BRCGS (global supply chain assurance), IFS and HACCP (food safety), CITEO (circular paper economy), RSPO (palm oil certificate), Rainforest Alliance, Halal and Kosher (dairy), BIO and NOP (EU and US organic), UTZ and FairTrade (EU and US).

Our charity is Cocoa for Schools, giving back to the community by assisting farmers in the cocoa-producing regions of Africa. Under the direction of our business partner, since 2010, Cocoa for Schools has paid above-market rates for cocoa with the surplus being administered locally to help build and renovate more than 416 classrooms in Tanzania. The target of our Cocoa for Schools project is to build, complete, or renovate in the next ten to twelve years around 2,100 classrooms and teachers' offices and to distribute around 430,000 school books. Beyond education, the project also assists farmers in a number of ways, including teaching agricultural skills, distributing new cocoa seedlings, and providing solar electricity generating devices. These diverse economic and educational programs seek to help enrich the lives of our esteemed cocoa-producing colleagues. Without them, the world would have no chocolate!

Chapter 20

HIDING BEHIND THE PILLAR

Lydia Knitzer was the CEO of General Mills in Minneapolis. She and I knew each other from when we had collaborated on testing co-bundled KC Chocolatier and Häagen-Dazs retail stores. General Mills owned Häagen-Dazs and had been looking for complementary products to add to their shop format so that Häagen-Dazs franchisees could make more money. Chocolates seemed like the perfect fit.

Lydia told me that she felt a European chocolate would go best with Häagen-Dazs because the public perception is of Häagen-Dazs as being a Scandinavian brand. She invited me to set up a booth at the annual Häagen-Dazs franchisee convention to introduce the KC Chocolatier product line. I created brochures explaining the remodeling budget required to make room for a chocolate display.

I had to decide how to forecast sales in order to demonstrate return on investment. I convinced Lydia to allocated money out of her CEO discretionary fund to build two co-bundled Häagen-Dazs/KC Chocolatier test stores as "proof of concept." That way, after a year of operating, we would have a set of actual books to be able to report to franchisees the profit potential from adding chocolate counters to existing ice cream stores.

We decided to interview some of Lydia's top franchisees at the conference to see which operators were the most ambitious. Lydia and I made up a questionnaire containing a lot of open-ended questions that could really draw out whether a candidate had in-depth industry knowledge. We made the process a lot like a college entrance exam because those Häagen-Dazs franchisees selected were benefiting from not only $100,000 in free store upgrades but from the increased profits to be enjoyed from selling KC Chocolatier products.

Two respondents that demonstrated the most passion for chocolate were store owners in Detroit and Phoenix. I flew to Detroit in the dead of winter to visit Twelve Oaks Mall. Bryce, the Häagen-Dazs store owner there, walked me through a tour of the mall. It turns out Twelve Oaks had Godiva and Sanders as year-round in-line tenants. Sanders is a Detroit-based chocolate company with a strong local following in the same vein as Fannie May in Chicago and Bissinger's in St. Louis. Sanders has a dedicated following in Michigan based on generations of brand-building.

I didn't like having to compete with Sanders, and I especially didn't want to go head-to-head in a mall with Godiva, which is something we never did. No matter how big a mall is, no shopping center can profitably support two Belgian chocolatiers. Our motto has been, "Go where Godiva isn't."

We met with the mall manager, a certified chocoholic who immediately started sampling from her complimentary box of chocolate. (I always carry free samples around, just in case.) The mall manager explained that she felt obligated to tell us, since she had a fiduciary duty to Bryce as a tenant, that the temporary leasing department had leased a kiosk to See's Chocolate for Christmas that year. We would be competing against three chocolate stores in Twelve Oaks mall!

I wanted the first test store to generate explosive sales figures, and that was not going to happen at Twelve Oaks. I told Bryce that General Mills, Häagen-Dazs, and KC Chocolatier all had to make money in order for the deal to make financial sense. Upon hearing that, Bryce pulled his power play. It turns out he owned all the Häagen-Dazs franchises in Hawaii. Bryce was in renewal negotiations with Lydia. He threatened to convert all the Hawaii stores to Ben & Jerry's if Lydia didn't choose him for the KC Chocolatier test. There is nothing like being blackmailed into a deal! Lydia said yes to Bryce and sent me on my way.

I got on a plane to visit the next candidate in Phoenix, worrying that the Detroit market in general might not be big enough or have the appropriate demographics for KC Chocolatier, let alone the Novi suburbs specifically, where Twelve Oaks is located. But the more I thought about it, Bryce won me over because he *wanted* to be a part of the excitement at KC Chocolatier.

Christian in Phoenix was catching us at the perfect time. His newest location in Biltmore Mall was under construction and due to open in a couple of months. Christian had taken over the lease of a former Godiva store that had closed! Godiva had decided not to renew the lease on their first-floor location next to Saks. I remembered that store because it had been one of my deals years before. It was a wide, shallow storefront with outdoor seating, not the typical narrow and deep configuration.

When Christian greeted me at the site with his contractor, he reminded me of what we had discussed during his interview, saying that he was looking forward to being the only chocolate retailer at

Biltmore. I had to remind Christian that the reason was obvious. Biltmore is an outdoor center. Phoenix is very hot in the summer. There was a reason why Godiva decided not to renew. This was going to be a seasonal location, dependent on winter snowbirds.

But as soon as I heard about Christian's unauthorized plan to add caramel apples and old-time penny candy to the concept, I excused myself and called Lydia. She went berserk and said, "I'm flying out right away." Naturally I had to extend my planned stay in Phoenix because there needed to be a balance of power. The highest-ranking executives at both companies needed to be relating directly to one another without communicating through intermediaries. That is something I've always been very aware of in any type of high-level negotiations. I couldn't leave town and hope she and Christian would work it out.

I explained to Christian that the General Mills board was very excited to launch the co-branded stores in the US. I mentioned that Lydia would be making a stop in Phoenix the next day, "on her way to Los Angeles." It had to sound casual and unplanned. "Lydia is flying to Phoenix to sign off with me on terms of the joint venture approved by General Mills' board," I said.

"Oh, no, she didn't just do that!" Christian replied, knowing she was pulling a power play. Having flown before on the General Mills private jet, a Falcon 8X, Christian knew that Lydia had pilots and crew on stand-by and could arrive in Phoenix tomorrow.

The next evening Lydia and I went to dinner at a chain restaurant, which is the only kind of restaurant I will eat at. While enjoying an appetizer, Lydia unexpectedly began asking a lot of questions about me. "How did you get your start in the chocolate business?" Lydia asked. I told her about having worked as the chocolate buyer at Bloomingdale's.

"And how did you wind up at Godiva?" she wanted to know. Throughout the meal, I repeated the often-told story of how I re-invented Godiva to create a juggernaut for global domination of the world's luxury chocolate industry.

Hearing this seemed to excite Lydia, not threaten her supremacy or bore her. I should have realized then and there that, unbeknownst to me, a light bulb was going off in Lydia's head! "What was she up to?" I thought to myself. Something strange was happening because never once that evening did we discuss business in the sense of her stores or her company, which I kept trying to direct the conversation towards. All we talked about was KC Chocolatier and Belgian chocolates.

The next day Lydia, Christian, and I met at the mall manager's conference room in the Biltmore executive offices. I spread out an elaborate display of all eighty kinds of chocolate we sold. The three of them were cutting chocolates in half, sampling each piece, trying to guess the flavors and the fillings, and then looking at me to see whether they were right.

I played my video, "A Tour of the Chocolate Factory," which is on KC Chocolatier's website. Lydia was impressed. Lydia had not realized until then that KC Chocolatier is a commercial venture. The factory I had contracted with to produce our chocolate cost €200 million and could produce about $500,000 worth of chocolate per hour. The plant had won the Laurel Award as the greenest factory in the Kingdom based on its green sustainability.

I just had to ask, "Lydia, what were you thinking, that I made the chocolate in my workroom? Like one of Santa's elves?"

She acted flabbergasted and answered in business-speak, saying, "Two hundred employees to work the line! That is some kind of payroll. And the raw materials costs! Purchasing takes on a life of its own, doesn't it?" Those responses confirmed she had been paying attention to details in the video. She had come to the realization we were peers—industry leaders who both could commiserate about running a multi-national conglomerate.

The next thing I knew, I was inviting Lydia to Brussels. "Tour the factory that produces for me," I said, "and taste the new chocolates in our development kitchen... and look at the packaging we have planned for your test stores." Lydia had her calendar out faster than you could say "Häagen-Dazs."

A week later we were in Belgium. As usual, first-time visitors are fascinated, especially with the chocolate aroma upon entering the building. Multiple production lines making bonbons take up acres of floor space, and five life-size, six-foot tall robots pull and pack orders for shipping on the loading dock.

The KC Chocolatier factory is a major manufacturing operation consisting of an enormous building on several levels. Enrobing lines and molding lines as long as a football field feature state-of-the-art automated machinery. Technicians operate and monitor various production lines using enormous touch-screen computers controlling speed, temperature, and machinery functions. At any given time during the day there are tens of thousands of pieces of chocolate working their way down one of the chocolate production lines, being automatically shaped, formed, drenched, jiggled, cut, boxed, and wrapped. Virtually the entire chocolate-making process is automated, with the exception of hand-garnishes and visual inspection for flaws.

KC Chocolatier's master chocolatier is Jules, the owner of the factory, my esteemed colleague, and a co-founder of the brand. Jules manages daily operations at the factory and provides tours himself; only he decides how much or how little of the chocolate-making process guests will get to see. Jules' secret recipes form the basis for KC Chocolatier's success. I could not wait to introduce Jules, so he could give Lydia a crash-course in luxury chocolate-making techniques.

As Jules and Lydia stood beside the high-speed molding line, he told her that at KC Chocolatier, "we don't talk about making chocolate; we do it." What he meant by that was getting to see our factory in motion is by special invitation only to our customers and guests, and that therefore there is no program to follow. The two of them could spend as much or as little time watching each production line in action as they wished, and they would be free to roam the building in any direction they felt like going. This was a typically busy day, so all production lines were in use with different lines producing dark, milk, and white chocolates.

The first thing Lydia noticed on the molding line was that it requires dozens of identical molds to produce one chocolate piece type because of the number of molds needed to equip the vertical conveyor belt as it rotates down from the ceiling towards the production line, allowing each mold to pass through a trough of melted chocolate before being flipped upside down to drip off excess chocolate as molds move towards the chilling chamber to harden the shells.

Jules took Lydia to the high-speed enrobing line where hundreds of pieces of finished chocolates per minute pass along on a moving rubber mat, surrounded by technicians placing a perfectly centered nut on top of each piece of chocolate. It is always a race for technicians seated on either side of the line to make sure that someone reaches every piece with a nut before each batch of chocolates moves past their garnishing zone. Each technician has a giant bowl of nuts to grab from, and working quickly, the garnishing team orchestrates their movements, so they don't get in each other's way.

Both the molding and enrobing lines feed onto a conveyor belt on an incline, taking chocolates up a ramp to the second-floor packaging department. The marvel of modern technology is KC Chocolatier's "laser vision" suction cup apparatus. Chocolates first fall into trays of eight little indentations, so pieces are lined up precisely. One at a time, trays move inside a clear acrylic box with red laser beams shooting down from above. The lasers are "seeing" the exact position of each tray of chocolates, and as they do, eight rubber suction cups lower to touch the top of all eight chocolates, picking them up and dropping the chocolates into a box without so much as even leaving a mark on the chocolates. This technology has sped up production more so than any other piece of equipment because in the old days, people had to pick up every finished chocolate by hand and pack them in a box, which was tedious and time consuming.

Lydia got to see where chocolate bars go on the second floor. Bars move into slots that swirl them around in a device that instantly wraps silver foil around each bar. Then the foil-covered chocolate bars drop onto a conveyor belt that runs through a packaging system, which folds a cardboard sleeve over every bar. These decorated sleeves are printed with identifying information such as the brand name, ingredients, and nutrition panel, which now look familiar to anyone who has ever shopped in the chocolate bar aisle at a supermarket. Twelve bars at a time are then boxed by employees into cartons.

I decided to meet up with Jules and Lydia late in the afternoon in the packaging display room, an interesting space for retailers who wish to examine a sample on display of every box we have ever created for all customers worldwide. While we never *say* who our customers are, people can see for themselves because retailers' names are printed on samples of their packaging from all over the world.

Since that concluded the tour, Jules had arranged a car to take Lydia and I back to the old town where our hotels were. We travelled on winding roads through picturesque villages on the outskirts of Brussels. Just she and I alone against the backdrop of church spirals, charming central town squares, and centuries-old brightly colored rowhouses provided the opportunity Lydia needed to enlist me in her plan. I was a captive for the ride as Lydia described her goal.

"Speaking on behalf of General Mills," Lydia began, "I intend to acquire KC Chocolatier." With a snap of her neck and a look at me with an unmistakable facial expression implying she was taking charge, and I better get used to her being the new boss, Lydia went on to say, "*You* are going to help me work out a deal with the factory."

What a twist in the saga! I didn't see that coming!

Lydia gave me instructions. I was expected to call Jules, the master chocolatier at the factory, when I got to the hotel and find out if he would agree to let Lydia assume the terms of my production contract. Then I was to report back to her by phone immediately. She'd be waiting for my call.

Just as we finished talking, our car pulled up at the Hotel Amigo. The driver let Lydia out, and I watched her stride triumphantly into the lobby, thinking it didn't surprise me at all that she'd be staying at the most expensive hotel in Belgium.

Less than five minutes later I arrived at my hotel. I only knew how to dial Belgian phone numbers from a land line because it is less confusing than having to know the country code and city code to dial from my US-based cell phone. As soon as I got to my room, I called Jules and asked, "How much should I sell KC Chocolatier for?"

"Say it's not for sale," Jules stated emphatically, as expected, adding "KC Chocolatier is your baby." But with a conspiratorial intonation in his voice, he added, "Why, did Lydia say something?" I felt like Dr. Henry Kissinger, negotiating a treaty. It was imperative to make it understood that my loyalty was to the *maître confiseur* who acted as my chocolate muse, creating whatever chocolates I could imagine.

"Lydia might try to approach you about taking over my contracts," I said. "She told me her plan the minute we got in the car. I just pulled up at the hotel and am calling you fast."

"I will only do that if you tell me that you two worked out a deal," Jules said, and hung up the phone.

My plan was just to blurt out a preposterous number to make it seem like we at least went through the exercise to get it over with. Obviously General Mills would never agree to some insane price, effectively putting it on their board to demur. By the time the General Mills' due diligence committee examined the books and determined the sale price could not be supported, the strike date would pass, and the deal would simply lapse.

I called Lydia, and she picked up. "Lydia, I'm so glad I reached you. I was in fact able to reach Jules. As you know, I never intended to sell. But, my deal with the factory would be transferable," I added.

My mind kept thinking of the old retail adage that banks will finance a retail store purchase for two times net earnings plus the underlying value of some goodwill. Knowing KC Chocolatier's top-line sales, and that I operate a network of stores, and that I have no debt, I explained that to Lydia off the top of my head.

"A multiplier of two times net profit of $2 million is $4 million. Add $1 million for goodwill and trade secrets, including the intellectual property of global logistics and the production contracts with the factory. I need $5 million, and we have a deal. Oh, and one more thing—it has to be an all-cash offer," I said, out-doing myself. (I didn't even have any paperwork with me to support these numbers.)

Imagine my surprise when Lydia didn't blink. "Fine," she said calmly, "I'll report to the board and see if we can get an LOI signed tomorrow while I'm here." Click. She hung up. Maybe I should've asked for ten million? What I thought was preposterous sounded just fine to her.

I called Jules and reported, "Lydia is messaging the board for permission to sign an LOI with me tomorrow. Their offer will be all cash." I specifically did not mention the dollar amount.

Very nonchalantly, he replied, "You better wait and see." Apparently, Jules thought nothing would come of it, and even if an offer did surface, Jules probably anticipated the transaction price to be a relatively small counter-offer.

The next day Lydia and I met in the prototype store built in the lobby of the factory. It is not a working store open to the public, but rather an example of the latest-and-best fixturing and merchandising guidelines for shops, being developed by the marketing department. Shopkeepers from around the world are able to see an example of what a KC Chocolatier shop looks like, set up according to best practices for various seasons, such as Valentine's and Easter.

Lydia and I each took a seat on two poofs, which are upholstered fun stools that float around low tables serving as children's seating. Not knowing my wicked sense of humor, Lydia did not bother to ask where the adult tables and chairs had been put since yesterday, but they were gone. Playing along, and without skipping a beat, Lydia opened her briefcase and wasted no time! "Brad, you positively must sell General Mills your business!" she said. "Our investment will take KC Chocolatier to the next level."

Knowing her offer was coming, based on our conversation the night before, I was ready, replying, "Well, Lydia, any good business comes at a good price. What could you offer?"

She slid the LOI across the little child-size table we were sitting around, taking great care to make sure the document was presented with the text facing my way, so I could read it easily.

"Five million euros, all cash. Our board has approved it," Lydia replied.

I had forgotten which country I was in and might have told Lydia "dollars," but Lydia thought I meant "euros" because we were in Europe, which were worth even more!

I glanced at her in complete disbelief, silently thinking to myself, "This is how easy it is to sell a company? There's not even any negotiation over the asking price? Or a request for supporting documents? Or any contingency clauses?"

Contrast the enormity of the offer against the miniscule kiddie table the deal was presented at. That has had the most impact on my memory from that day. In my mind I picture the juxtaposition of two of the business world's industry leaders sitting on little children's leather upholstered stools. Suddenly I understood the irony of what I had done. The "poofs" were designed with no sharp edges to protect youngsters, and this meeting did not have a hard edge to it at all now that the money was doing the talking!

Without so much as saying a word, I removed the Mont Blanc pen from my Zegna blue shirt, signed two copies, and slid them back across the table to Lydia with a knowing look. "Well then," she pronounced with a satisfied grin, "have Jules show me everything about how my chocolates are made."

Jules and Lydia practically skipped through the building that day, like two school children on a field trip to the chocolate factory. As for me, I'd seen it all before, and sat in Jules's office at his big desk reading the National Enquirer and using his private Nespresso machine, imagining that Lydia might transfer me to Brussels, and this could be my office once I was on the General Mills payroll.

Lydia got to visit the research lab, where the team was deciding on the shape for a new key lime and green tea dark chocolate that I was preparing to launch soon. She brought me three pieces to eat in the office, saying that next they were going to the production floor to watch KC Chocolatier's newest product line being made. That day, filled chocolate bars were being crafted. (I had suggested creating chunky chocolate bars with a thin chocolate shell surrounding soft truffle fillings.)

After all the excitement of that afternoon, I left for my hotel, so I could pack, and suggested we meet for a drink at Lydia's hotel before I left for the airport. Jules met us at 5:00, and I ordered champagne (for them) and Evian (for me, since I don't drink). "A toast," I said, "to our deal." Upon clinking glasses, I wanted to discuss Lydia's ideas for growing KC Chocolatier, so I asked Lydia a question, "What are your plans for my brand?"

Lydia's instantaneous answer was, "Oh, we'll be phasing out the KC Chocolatier brand. All we want is your factory contract, so we can manufacture our candies in Belgium and be able to advertise them as 'Made in Belgium.'"

When I heard that, my face twisted into a sour expression, and it felt like steam was about to come out of my vents. I said, "Jules, could I just see you for a moment please ... over there," while kissing Lydia on both cheeks to bid her *adieu,* saying "I have to run, *bon voyage,* enjoy your flight back to Minneapolis."

We went to hide behind a marble pillar in the lobby of the hotel where the bar was. I pulled my copy of the letter of intent out of my jacket pocket and ripped it up! Then I handed the torn pieces to Jules. "Go tell *that woman* the deal is off," I scowled, throwing up my hands.

"Brad, you don't want to cancel this deal. *You need five million cash*!" Jules protested.

"No, I don't!" I proclaimed as I stormed out towards my waiting car idling in front.

As Jules tried to chase me out to the *porte-cochere* to convince me to change my mind, I found myself standing on the cobblestones gazing at the illuminated red taillights of the hotel's Bentley.

It occurred to me that the shape of the taillights looked eerily familiar. Then it struck me—Jules had designed KC Chocolatier's newest mold in the shape of a Bentley's taillights. The new green tea and key lime dark chocolate resembled a Bentley Mulsanne's characteristic three-hatch-mark motif. Revelations like this seemed to strike at the oddest moments. I felt like I was entering the "Twilight Zone" between my mind processing that I was right but realizing that if Jules wanted me to know where his ideas came from, he would have told me.

I left Jules to do the dirty work. That's how it always is: I make the person who I think created the mess, clean it up.

Jules told me he went back in and apologized to Lydia for having to step away. "There's been a change of plans," he started out saying to Lydia, "It seems Brad changed his mind. He's not selling."

Lydia tried insisting that a deal is a deal. "General Mills is in possession of a fully executed, legally binding contract," she said, referring to the letter of intent.

"Not anymore," Jules responded, dropping the torn-up pieces of the contract on the table.

Every time I think about it, I am relieved I found out about Lydia's plans before the money was transferred. I talked with Bryce and Christian who said that Lydia called them to say the co-branding test was canceled. She didn't even tell me directly. Häagen-Dazs went with Rocky Mountain Chocolate instead.

Chapter 21

WHEN YOU THINK YOU'VE HEARD IT ALL

I had my chance to sell and didn't. The opportunity came up because General Mills observed the same phenomenon that I had: KC Chocolatier had been founded as a spontaneous reaction to my personal astonishment that there was no chocolate made in Belgium that was nationally distributed in the US at that time. This single realization was actionable because as I proved at Godiva, many Americans probably believed there were several Belgian chocolate brands available in the United States.

Belgium, France, and Switzerland are the three countries with the world's highest per-capita consumption of chocolate. But even in Switzerland and France, Belgian chocolate is the bestseller, outselling those countries' domestically produced brands. I was fearlessly certain there was a way for Belgian chocolate to outsell American-made luxury chocolate in the US. But I had to have a plan for how to thread the needle, creating awareness within my budget.

The solution was to fall back on my tried-and-true business format of opening branded KC Chocolatier retail stores. I decided to focus on creating a shop concept which would establish credibility, complementing wholesale operations. I knew from experience that given time, both channels would snowball into dual revenue streams, which would provide consistent sales. Opening KC Chocolatier branded retail stores is what enabled my marketing to *speak from a position of authority based on my chocolate heritage*:

- Godiva is a marketing company
- Leonidas is a chocolate company
- KC Chocolatier is a financial company

KC Chocolatier finances the cost of building stores by licensing independent owners to operate them. KC Chocolatier finances the cost of shipping large orders by obtaining credit insurance which provides an advance against each PO.

KC Chocolatier combines the best of both Leonidas and Godiva – great chocolate, well marketed. We have financed the sale of thousands of metric tonnes of chocolate in our first fifteen years in business. (The industry measures output in tonnes because sales are reported in euros per kilo in Belgium versus in dollars per pound in the U.S.)

As the vendor of record at all retail chains we supply, I have worked to guarantee adherence to US labeling and nutritional compliance requirements. I have served as KC Chocolatier's FSVP ("Food Safety Verification Program") officer, the liaison between US customs and the factory. None of the three brands I've managed has ever had a recall. I believe there is no such thing as a coincidence, since President Donald J. Trump's staff approached me about being considered to serve as US Ambassador to Belgium. I politely declined having my name submitted for Congressional approval, knowing that without me at the helm daily, KC Chocolatier would have been "on the road to nowhere."

President Trump had been paying close attention to the Kingdom since the Zaventem Airport bombing in early 2016. At 5:04 a.m. on March 24, 2016, Trump tweeted, "Do you all remember how beautiful and safe a place Brussels was. [sic] Not anymore, it is from a different world! U.S. must be vigilant and smart!"

Trump's tweet was in response to the March 22 Brussels airport bombing. I already knew what happened that day because I was there at Brussels Airport when the bombs started going off! I will never forget my harrowing experience. I was en route to Los Angeles after meetings at the factory. I had arrived at the international terminal early the morning of March 22. First, I went to the check-in counter to check luggage. Then I walked past the gift shops to go through security and was at the airline lounge when the first bomb went off near the gift shops. The entire building shook. Alarms began to sound. Moments later, a second bomb went off at the ticket counter where I had just checked in. The roof fell in from the power of the blast. Airport employees told all the passengers to evacuate the building as deadly shards of glass rained down from shattered skylights.

I did not know what to do in the chaos and had to think fast because steel girders that had been holding up the building were twisting and bending where the roof used to be. My exit was blocked; I could not go back out the way I came in because that part of the building was in flames. Suddenly the gas line exploded, causing the ground to shake like a 10.0 earthquake, violently throwing me to the ground. I got up and pushed an emergency exit bar that said, "Press here in case of emergency." The door opened to a stairway down to the tarmac. I found himself almost underneath a departing jumbo jet, trying not to get sucked into an engine by the powerful force of thrust created by the turbines. Thousands of people were fleeing out of all the exits onto to the concrete apron.

I made it on foot to a field between some runways but did not go any farther in case planes were landing. A bus stopped, and the driver picked us up and dropped us off by a chain link fence on the other side of the airport by the freeway. Cars started stopping on the shoulder of the highway to give people rides as the news was all over the radio. I wound up somewhere and made my way to the central train station, trying to figure out the Brussels subway system to get back to my hotel. Fortunately, I was not hurt.

Ever since that day, I have not gone back to Belgium.

I have since developed new businesses within the US. The litmus test for deciding to expand into complementary businesses was whether doing so could leverage my existing relationships with KC Chocolatier's store network.

First, I decided to create a division to supply chocolate boxes to the stores that were *already* buying chocolate from me. I created distinctive keepsake packaging specifically designed for hand-packing KC Chocolatier at the point of sale. After all, is it not possible to sell bulk chocolate to a customer at the candy counter without having a box to put it in. My new division, "Chocolate-In-The-Box" makes a very specific type of hand-painted, hand-glittered, hand-decorated collectible box featuring seasonal vintage images found in the public domain. A unique and proprietary non-photographic process is used for transferring the images onto each box, giving the impression that the box and the art are one. The result has customers thinking that the box was manufactured with the image printed on it. The secret process offers shopkeepers the flexibility to place minimum order quantities of three to six boxes per design, enabling them to stock hundreds of boxes with different images. Offering the shopping public a variety of boxes lets store owners up-sell for a surcharge over the normal offering of a standard KC Chocolatier logo box. I envision a time in the near future when I will begin selling "Chocolate-In-The-Box" packaging to other companies needing customized gift box solutions.

Another new US division is a sales office searching for licensees to open KC Chocolatier stores. This means I oversee a group of salespeople selling *licenses* to sell chocolates as opposed to salespeople selling chocolate. That is a business I have not been in since owning Kelly's Coffee.

These licensees have since taken over responsibility for calling on large retail chains who might place wholesale orders. That way individual store owners share in the profits.

Recently I joined such a licensee calling on a client in Milwaukee. The head of procurement, who was young, wore green hair, and dressed in a way I cannot describe, was a daughter of the founder whose business card read rather nebulously, "Chief Thinker." She did have clout because everything went so smoothly as orders were placed for several pallets a month. The buyer was ecstatic every time her stores sold out.

Eventually the buyer called me personally and with glee in her lyrical voice, declared, "We're doing so well with your product we'll have to drop it!"

Just when you think you've heard it all, I blurted out, "I'm confused. Please clarify. Do you mean you want to order different chocolates from us?"

"No, we're going to knock you off and make chocolate ourselves cheaper," she admitted proudly, as if we had been outsmarted.

My industry sources tipped me off that this buyer ordered Chinese chocolates. She took a tour of "Factory A," which is shiny and bright, built to European standards, but the orders are actually produced in "Factory B," which buyers never see because it is not presentable. That is how the manufacturer gets the price down. I don't think I want to know what Chinese chocolates taste like.

Sometimes I have to do what I don't want to do, which in this case meant approaching the above retailer's direct competitor. I must maintain my market share in any given trade area. Fortunately, since I own the company, I could drop the price as low as we needed to go to land the account.

Financially, the chocolate business affords such flexibility in pricing. The production cycle is predictable. Manufacturing does not require extensive capital investment compared to other industries. Turnaround time from ordering raw materials to taking money in the cash register is one short season. Retained earnings provide sufficient cash flow for most of the year's continuing operations. I only need to draw down from a revolving credit line once per year during summer to gear up for Christmas production. The relatively low cost of borrowing is factored into the gross margins.

There is still a first time for everything, apparently, as I learned recently. I always try to be prepared to expect the unexpected in retailing. But I never imagined that a prominent US department store chain could ask for markdown money before their chocolate even shipped!

I protested to the buyer that markdown money is for slow-selling merchandise. I wanted to know how he could be thinking that our hundred gram decoratively glittered Easter chocolate bars were to be considered a slow seller, when the shipment hadn't even hit the warehouse yet—let alone made its way out to the branches?

The conversation was mind-bogglingly premature, and I told the buyer so.

I quickly got to the bottom of what was really happening: This chain wanted to lower the retail price from twelve to ten dollars. The buyer was looking for a way to accomplish this because he did not have any markdown money left in his Easter budget. Big companies leave a paper trail with every decision, making it complicated for a buyer wanting to do something.

The PO had been written and signed off at a cost and gross margin reflecting twelve dollars retail. Internally, he had no way to override the PO and have the warehouse ticket the chocolate at ten dollars. So, he got creative, took out a piece of blank paper, and made up his own new "official form," which he titled "Markup Cancellation." Instead of taking sixty points, as reflected on the PO, he "cancelled" on paper the "extra" ten points above the budgeted fifty-point margin goal that the candy department is reviewed on. The scheme worked.

As this book went to print, the buyer was promoted to vice president. I presume that was due to his creative approach to problem solving. We'll never know, but one of "Brad's Rules" still holds true after all these years: His assistant got promoted and is now the new buyer.

Another one of "Brad's Rules" is to never schedule chocolate meetings in the mornings. People do not want to sample chocolate before lunch. Potential clients often have to try it to buy it, which is why my team takes chocolate to every meeting.

The most important of "Brad's Rules" is that the person responsible for an organization has to keep the pendulum swinging. My intention for joining Godiva had been for the North American division to overtake the European division as measured in sales and profits. While the market was here to grow the US executives' sphere of power and influence within the Godiva worldwide organization, the will to do it had not previously been omnipresent before I came on the scene. I made a conscious decision that the folks in Belgium would someday take direction from us, not the other way around, which had been the status quo and was what the Brussels team felt to inherently be their natural station in life, as the cradle of chocolate. I am referring to control over fundamental core issues about finances and other resources, which impacted choices about which types of chocolates to make, what kind of packaging to create, and how Godiva would be advertised in the marketplace. As history proves, I succeeded in swinging the pendulum to the point that Godiva US leadership decided to sell the company.

And now, I reveal that my intention for writing this book is to prepare shoppers for a new world order in chocolate. In the next few years, KC Chocolatier will swing the pendulum of the global chocolate industry by launching an entirely new category of assorted chocolates. These will be so-called "modern chocolates" produced in bright colors. KC Chocolatier will be the first to achieve commercial scale production of all-natural, vegan "modern chocolates" using a soon-to-be-announced domestic manufacturing facility. Contemporary fillings might include blueberry cheesecake, strawberry and balsamic vinegar, tahini date with sesame, mint lemonade, and other bold flavor profiles aimed at satisfying multicultural palettes.

The tipping point has arrived; a US-based manufacturer will assume a leadership position in the super premium chocolate category.

Customers should be excited! For you see, the most important thing that matters to me is for my customers to be delighted.

Sensational packaging will make a dazzling new gift presentation. Holiday pieces will feature seasonal artwork and contain limited-edition fillings. Our "modern chocolate" offering will be first-to-market, keeping my organization at the forefront as the preferred supplier for fine chocolate.

The timing is good because the pendulum has swung in the corporate-gifting world too, comparing today versus thirty years ago—chocolate companies cannot survive without strong corporate orders. It used to be that wine, champagne, and liquor were the most prestigious corporate gifts to give at Christmas, followed by fine chocolates. Now, chocolate seems to have overcome liquor and wine as the preferred corporate gift, based on reports from my stores. Businesses have grown more sensitive about the consumption of alcohol and companies of all sizes recognize the multigenerational appeal of luxury chocolate—the entire family may enjoy it. KC Chocolatier will have the technology to print company logos on "modern chocolates."

What else might the future hold for KC Chocolatier? Possibly a diversification into offering a rewards program and a credit card. We might participate in a REIT to open stores in owned locations rather than leasing as a tenant. I foresee a future in nontraditional distribution channels including TV retail, delivery through apps, and online sales via Facebook, Etsy, and Instagram. Line extensions into hot chocolate and cookies could happen. The litmus test is whether these touch points would help elevate KC Chocolatier in the minds of the public. If the answer is "no," then the other alternative is always to create a secondary brand, something I wanted to do at both Godiva and Leonidas. As Brandy, my Godiva rep in Miami, used to say all those years ago, "It's on my list."

I would like to close with my message to the two hundred global staff working at KC Chocolatier's stores by saying, *thank you* for constantly delighting customers with excellent service. It doesn't surprise me that people enjoy their careers at KC Chocolatier because a chocolate store is a fun place to work.

And to my esteemed Licensees here and abroad, who live and breathe the KC Chocolatier brand daily, please enjoy the satisfaction of knowing that I am aware of all that you do, and if it wasn't for you, my vision could not have become a reality. Congratulations to you for opening such beautiful stores. I want to point out to readers that seven Licensees have been with me since the days of Leonidas (and two since Godiva). These are my closest group of advisors.

I did accomplish my goal of creating a space that had never existed in this world before I came along. Retail used to be "all business." There was no fun in shopping. I decided to bring joy into people's hearts through the experiential, multi-sensory habitats that I called, "Godiva," "Kelly's Coffee," "Leonidas," and "KC Chocolatier." I am proud to say that I have noticed many brands trying to imitate my formula. Some do it better than others, but all are on the right track. And to the shareholders of my brands who went along for a ride on my journey, I say, "Bravo!" Thank you for entrusting your precious assets to me. It was an honor and a privilege.

GODIVA GAME

Your Age in Chocolate

1. Pick the number of times a week that you would like to eat chocolate (more than once but less than 10)
2. Multiply this number by 2 (the pieces are small)
3. Add 5
4. Multiply it by 50
5. If you have already had your birthday this year add, add the number in column A below
6. If you haven't already had your birthday this year, add the number in column B below
7. Now subtract the four-digit year that you were born
8. You should have a three-digit number
9. The first digit of this was your original number from line 1
10. (how many times you want to have chocolate each week)
11. The next two numbers are YOUR AGE! (Godiva says so)
12. By providing your friends the numbers from the columns below for line 6 based on the year, you can tell people "This is the only year it will work!"

	A	B
Year	If You've Had Your Birthday	If You Haven't Yet
2024	1774	1773
2025	1775	1774
2026	1776	1775
2027	1777	1776
Next years	1777 +1 for each year	"A"-1

Line 5 example playing the Godiva game in 2025:

If you have already had your birthday this year add, 1775

If you haven't already had your birthday this year, add 1774

LEONIDAS PUZZLE

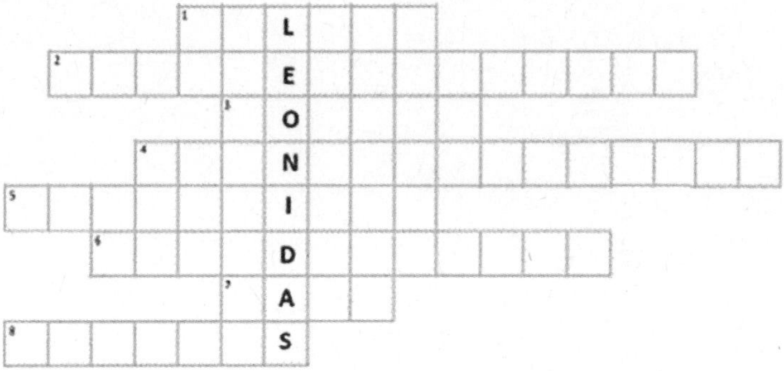

1. Chocolatier based in Liege featuring a distinctive orange logo
2. Winner of forty chocolate medals, opened his namesake boutique on the Sablon in 1997
3. Global chocolate brand named after the Earl of Coventry's wife
4. Operates thirty stores following its acquisition of Cornet de la Toison d'Or
5. Greek confectioner founded this chocolate house in Ghent in 1923
6. Chocolatier founded in 1986, with a blue and brown color scheme in stores
7. Belgian Royal Warrant holder since 1942, purveyor to the King and Queen of Belgium
8. Exhibited at the World Expo in Brussels in 1958, representing the Belgian chocolate industry

ANSWERS

Answers: 1. Galler 2. Pierre Marcolini 3. Godiva 4. Cornet Port Royal 5. Daskalides 6. Jeff de Bruges 7 Mary 8. Neuhaus

ACKNOWLEDGMENTS

To Wendy Keller
Keller Media

To Debby Englander
Post Hill Press

To Cheri Brulport
Macy's

To Nancy Robbins, Rob Skubiak, and Liz Amberger
Godiva Chocolatier

To Mike White and Debbie White
Kelly's Coffee

To Cathy Altazin
Air France

To AnneMie van de Velde and Steve Johnson
Leonidas Chocolate

To Fons Maex
KC Chocolatier

And to Scott and Heather Peisner